A4
A8

THE ARCTIC VOYAGES OF MARTIN FROBISHER

THE ARCTIC VOYAGES
OF MARTIN FROBISHER

An Elizabethan Adventure

ROBERT McGHEE

Canadian Museum of Civilization

University of Washington Press
Seattle & London

© Canadian Museum of Civilization, 2001

ISBN 0-7735-2235-2

Legal deposit third quarter 2001
Bibliothèque nationale du Québec

Printed in Singapore on acid-free paper

Published in the United States of America by the University of Washington Press, PO Box 50096,
Seattle, WA 98145-5096.

ISBN 0-295-98163-6

This book was designed by David LeBlanc and typeset in 12/15 Centaur MT

Contents

PREFACE

THIS BOOK IS THE RESULT OF THE RESEARCH, advice, support, and friendship of an extremely large number of people with whom I have worked during my ten-year association with the Frobisher story. The association began with archaeological research on the Frobisher sites in Arctic Canada and continued through involvement with the Meta Incognita Committee and the development of the exhibition *Inuit and Englishmen: The Nunavut Voyages of Martin Frobisher.* Each of these projects engaged the talent and commitment of many people, of whom I can name only a few.

My interest in the Frobisher archaeological sites was first kindled by the enthusiasm of the late Walter Kenyon, when he visited Jim Tuck and me in Newfoundland while preparing for his 1974 expedition to Kodlunarn Island. It would be sixteen years before Tuck and I actually saw the island, and then it was Tuck who provided the knowledge and direction that produced useful results from our 1990 and 1991 visits. I continue to be grateful for Jim's friendship and support through these and other experiences. Of the people who worked with us during those seasons, special mention should go to Lee Jablonski and Jean Pilon, whose volunteer efforts in the surface and subsurface mapping of Kodlunarn Island were extremely valuable. Réginald Auger, Donald Hogarth, and Rob MacIntosh also provided essential assistance in the fields of archaeology, geology, and botany.

Throughout the 1990s Stephen Alsford supplied a valuable link to the work of the Meta Incognita Committee, which advised on research related to the Frobisher voyages. Thomas H.B. Symons and the late William E. Taylor Jr coordinated this unwieldy organization to useful ends. Charles Arnold, of the Prince of Wales Northern Heritage Centre, and Douglas Stenton, of the Inuit Heritage Trust, were

committee members who were always available to hear the concerns of the archaeologists associated with the project.

The development of this book is intimately tied to the *Inuit and Englishmen*
exhibition at the Canadian Museum of Civilization, and I use this opportunity to
thank those who contributed to that project. The exhibit benefited greatly from the
talents of designer Sunniva Geuer and the work of many Museum employees.
Special mention should be made of Caroline Marchand (conservation), Laurie
Schroeder (video production), and the model makers who produced a convincing
reconstruction of the Fenton watchtower on Kodlunarn Island, as well as a fascinating model of the island as it may have appeared in August 1578. Others who
made essential contributions to the exhibit include Alootook Ippellie, Bernard
Allaire, Réginald Auger, Francis Back, Donald Hogarth, Janet McGrath (Tamalik),
Nick Newbery, and Claude Paulette. Stephen Alsford and Sandra Hamel produced
an outstanding Internet web site related to the exhibition.

The exhibit depended heavily on borrowed objects, many of which are illustrat-
ed in this book. Of the many people who helped in this effort, I wish especially to
thank Mary Clapinson, Keeper of Western Manuscripts, Bodleian Library; Hazel
Forsyth, Curator (Post-Medieval), Museum of London; Anthony Griffiths, Keeper, Department of Prints and Drawings, British Museum; Gloria Clifton, Curator
of Navigational Instruments, National Maritime Museum; P.J. Porter, Head of
Manuscript Loans, British Library; Ian Friel, Littlehampton Museum; Katherine
Golden and William Fitzhugh, Smithsonian Institution; and Mima Kapches, of the
Royal Ontario Museum. I wish also to express my special thanks to Robert Baldwin, who very kindly introduced me to the mysteries and some of the more fascinating holdings of the British Museum and the British Library, and to Sir Ian
Gourlay, who hospitably introduced me to the National Maritime Museum and
the other resources in Greenwich.

Like any treatment of a complex historical event, this book is heavily dependent on
the work of other researchers. Many of these scholars continue to actively contribute
to knowledge related to the Frobisher voyages, and I wish to make special mention of
how useful I have found their work. I am particularly indebted to the contributors to

three books published in association with the Meta Incognita Project: *Archaeology of the Frobisher Voyages*, edited by William W. Fitzhugh and Jacqueline S. Olin; Donald Hogarth's *Martin Frobisher's Northwest Venture, 1576–1581: Mines, Minerals & Metallurgy*; and *Meta Incognita: A Discourse of Discovery*, edited by Thomas H.B. Symons. The last, a collection of historical papers and essays, in particular the excellent chapters by James McDermott that comprise the central part of a biography of Martin Frobisher, were invaluable. Elizabeth Hulse is thanked for her excellent editing of the manuscript, and Lisa Leblanc for her assistance in production.

Finally, I must express my gratitude to Patricia Sutherland, without whose advice and support I could never have survived the decade of our association with Martin Frobisher.

Editorial note: The Frobisher voyages are well documented in numerous logs, journals, and other records that were originally published during the late sixteenth century. These accounts provide an invaluable sense of the intellectual, religious, and political atmosphere in which the adventures took place, and numerous excerpts from these early publications are reproduced in the following pages. In including such extracts, I have attempted to reproduce the original text while taking the liberty of making a few changes to Elizabethan spelling, which is liable to baffle contemporary readers; these have primarily meant the substitution of *s* for the sixteenth-century letter that modern readers find confusingly similar to *f* and the interchange of the letters *u* and *v* to their current usage. No attempt has been made to standardize the haphazard and at times bizarre spelling of the Elizabethan authors, and readers should be warned that the names of people, ships, and places will be found in several forms in the excerpts from original texts. Thus the ship that we call *Aid* appears in the text as *Aid, Ayde, Ayd,* and *Aide.* With this caution, I hope that readers will find that the difficulty of deciphering these texts is compensated by the enjoyment of savouring this early and vigorous form of the English language.

THE ARCTIC VOYAGES OF MARTIN FROBISHER

Preamble

July 14, 1576

THEY WERE FIVE WEEKS OUT OF ENGLAND, driving through a storm on the icy edge of the world, when a sudden blast knocked the *Gabriel* on her side. The helmsman frantically tried to turn the tiny ship into the wind which pinned her down, but the rudder had lifted clear of the surface and took no purchase. Water poured over the side, roaring into the hatches as the wind drove the vessel across the waves and the crew clung frozen in despair. Only the captain acted, scrambling along the almost horizontal upper sides, casting off lines to spill wind from the sails, commanding the crew into action to cut away the mizzen-mast and the broken foreyard, and then preventing them from doing the same to the mainmast. Finally, the *Gabriel* rose sluggishly, heavy with sea water but steering slowly off the wind. A tangle of broken rigging and sodden sails, she wallowed before the storm through the rest of the day and all the following night, while the captain restored order and set the men to pumping the ship dry.

Martin Frobisher had experienced many frightening situations at sea, but few can have been as desperate as this. The two other ships in his fleet had disappeared, almost certainly sunk with all hands. The only land that the expedition had encountered in the weeks since they left England was a range of glacier-covered mountains, and even this forbidding landscape was protected by so much grinding sea ice that their attempts to get ashore had been rebuffed. Now partially disabled, in fog and storm and massive islands of drifting ice, they were sailing into an unknown sea where they would meet no other ship. Their compass now pointed far from north, there were no stars to be seen in the bright sky of summer nights, and the sun was mostly obscured by fog and cloud. Even if the mariners could navigate, they could

The Arctic region in Gerhard Mercator's 1569 map of the world (courtesy National Archives of Canada; G/1026/.M47/1891/folio atlas)

not avoid the unknown hazards that undoubtedly lay ahead — hidden shoals, a sudden rocky coast, piratical savages, or the dangerous conditions of weather, waves, and ice peculiar to this strange region of the world.

As the storm lessened and the ship was returned to sailing order, Frobisher must have been tempted to drop his search for a sea passage to the north of the New World. By continuing to limp southwards the expedition could find help among the large European fleets working the cod-fishing banks and whaling waters off Newfoundland. The passage to England could be made before the wind, in known waters and in warmer conditions at lower latitudes. The night that followed the storm may have been the most decisive moment in the adventures of Elizabethan mariners in what was to become Arctic Canada. We do not know what doubts Frobisher may have faced that night, but we do know his decision, as reported by Michael Lok in his narrative of the voyage. The captain was

yet still determined alone to follow his enterprise and voyage according to commission to the uttermost of his power. And rather to make a sacrifice onto God of his lyfe than to return home withowt the discovery of Kathay except by compulsion of extreme force and necessity. And so returned to the course of his way toward the Land of Labrador, according to commission. And by fayre and by fowle on the xxixth day of July the capitayn himself first had sight of a new land of marveilous great heith. The headland wherof he named Elizabeth Foreland in memory of the Quene's Majestie.

The landfall was Resolution Island, the most eastern outlier of Arctic North America. For the first time, this vast northern region would enter the consciousness of Europe. Over the next three summers it would be the scene of an adventure involving the largest Arctic expedition ever assembled, the first attempt by the English to establish a settlement in the New World, and the first major gold-mining fraud in North American history. Frobisher's claim of possession would establish English interest in northern North America, and it was the first step in the eventual establishment of English sovereignty over the northern half of the American continents.

One

LODESTONES, UNICORNS, AND PERPETUAL DAYLIGHT

TO SIXTEENTH-CENTURY EUROPEANS, THE ARCTIC was as distant and fantastic as another planet. It was imagined as a region of frozen seas and perpetual daylight, the circling sun illuminating a landscape that mysteriously attracted the compass needle and from which occasional travellers brought tales of ice and pygmies, the skins of great white bears, and the horns of unicorns. The map of the Arctic regions drawn in 1569 by the celebrated Flemish geographer Gerhard Mercator assembled much of contemporary European knowledge about the area. The North Pole was depicted as an immense mountain surrounded by an open sea. Four northward-flowing and seasonally frozen channels divided a circumpolar continent, forming a massive whirlpool that swirled around the polar mountain before draining into the interior of the earth. This continent was separated from Eurasia and America by a broad sea containing islands large and small, including a mountain of iron that protruded from the sea on the opposite side of the Pole from Europe and was the attractor of magnetic compass needles.

The information on which Mercator based his map had gradually accumulated since classical times, beginning with the voyage of the Greek trader Pytheas, who had sailed to a distant northern land named Thule. There the sun remained in the sky at night, and his ship was prevented from sailing farther by a strange phenomenon that caused earth, sea, and air to congeal together. Many of the geographical concepts included in the Mercator map, however, came from two more recent and dubious sources. The first was a mysterious book titled *Inventio Fortunata*, which has not been seen since the sixteenth century. The *Inventio* was apparently a description of the Arctic regions between latitude 54° and the Pole, and it was said to have been

presented to Edward III of England by a learned friar from Oxford who had travelled widely in the Arctic during the mid-1300s. This monk has been dubiously
identified as Nicholas of Lynn, who, it has been suggested, visited the Norse settlements in Greenland during the 1360s. Here he may have learned the elements of
traditional Norse geography that were described in the *Inventio* and later appeared
on Mercator's map: the polar continent divided by "indrawing seas," the "Scrael-
ings" and "Pygmies" who inhabited this continent, and the whirlpool or maelstrom
of Norse cosmology.

Mercator's other source was a map that had been published in Venice in 1558 and
purported to illustrate North Atlantic lands discovered by the brothers Zeno during a series of voyages which had occurred during the 1380s. The Zeno map was a
fraudulent pastiche of information from other sixteenth-century sources, and its
primary effect was to clutter the northwestern Atlantic with several imaginary islands: Estland, Frisland, Icaria, Estotiland, and Drogeo, among others. The fact that
the Zeno chart could be accepted by a geographer as well informed as Mercator
demonstrates the low level of European knowledge relating to the north. The
accompanying text peopled these imaginary lands with cannibals, warriors, and
Christian monastic colonies, reflecting the European view that the Arctic was not a
barren desert but a region that could support thriving civilizations. The French
cosmographer Guillaume Postel encapsulated this view in his statement that "here
under and aboute the Pole is beste habitation for man, and that they ever have continuall daye, and know not what night or darkenesse meaneth."

This concept of habitable land in the far north tempered the tales of frozen seas,
iron mountains, giant whirlpools, pygmies, and perpetual day. The knowledge that
some of these far northern regions did support European settlements must have
been current in at least some of the seaports of northern Europe. Iceland, on the
edge of the frozen sea, had for seven centuries been home to Norse farmers and
fishermen who had successfully established the world's first republic. English fishermen, traders, and pirates had frequented the coasts of Iceland since the early fifteenth century, and considerable commerce had developed between the two
countries. Several days' sail farther to the northwest, in an even more isolated and

extreme environment, five centuries of Norse had established settlements along the southwestern coast of Greenland. The Greenlandic colonies faded from history at some time during the fifteenth century, but the remains of stone-built cathedrals and monasteries along the shores of uninhabited fjords may be reflected in stories such as those of the fabulous Zeno brothers. Although recorded voyages to Norse Greenland ended in 1410, it seems likely that contact with Europe continued after that date. In historian Gwyn Jones's words, "we may conclude that an occasional ship was storm-driven to Greenland of whose fate we hear nothing, and that resolute and high-handed English skippers in the fifteenth century sailed into Greenland waters for fish and sea-beasts, for honest trade where it offered, and for plunder where it lay to hand." Sixteenth-century Norwegian priests, Icelandic historians, and English sailors must all have had some knowledge of this strange and distant outpost of European civilization.

Vilhjalmur Stefansson, an Arctic explorer of the early twentieth century, thought it certain that the sixteenth-century English venturers into the northwestern Atlantic not only knew of Norse Greenland but had access to actual Norse sailing directions to reach that locality. The most likely version of these directions is thought to be that recorded by Ivar Bardarson, a church official who was sent to Greenland in 1341 by the bishop of Bergen in Norway, in order to report on conditions in that distant colony (and perhaps more importantly, to collect church taxes or tithes). Over the following years Bardarson travelled widely among the Norse Greenlandic settlements, and on his return to Europe, he wrote the most complete description of the country at that time. About sailing to Greenland, he reported:

Those who wish to sail directly from Bergen to Greenland, without touching Iceland, should steer directly west until they are opposite Rehkjanes in Iceland, at which time they should be twelve miles offshore. Then, following the westward course, they should arrive under high land at Greenland. This is called Hvarf. A day before reaching Hvarf the navigator should see another cliff, named Hvitserk. Between these two mountains, named Hvarf and Hvitserk, lies a promontory named Herjolfsnes where there is a harbour named Sand. Norwegians and traders land there customarily.

Herjolfsness was the most easterly of the Norse settlements, located just to the west of Cape Farewell at Greenland's southern tip. Hvitserk (White Shirt) must have been one of the heavily glaciated mountains on the rugged and uninhabitable south-eastern coast of Greenland. Bardarson's original report was in Latin, but it had been translated into German by 1560 and into Dutch shortly thereafter. As we shall see in the following chapter, geographical information and instruction was provided to Martin Frobisher by the learned scholar John Dee, who travelled widely in the Low Countries and had an extensive acquaintance among the leading geographers of that area. It seems reasonable to believe that Stefansson may be correct in supposing that Frobisher was following the old sea roads of the Norse into the Arctic regions.

The reactions of sixteenth-century English sailors to the Arctic environment is by turn amusing, appalling, and difficult to understand. When Martin Frobisher's crew found the body of a narwhal on a Baffin Island beach in 1577, they tested its magical powers as an antidote to poison and declared it to be a unicorn: "On this West shoare we found a dead fishe floating, whiche had in his nose a horne streight and torquet, of lengthe two yardes lacking two ynches, being broken in the top, where we might perceive it hollowe, into which some of our Saylers putting Spiders, they presently dyed. I sawe not the tryall hereof, but it was reported unto me of a trueth: by the vertue whereof, we supposed it to be a sea Unicorne" (Dionyse Settle's account of the 1577 voyage). The spirally grooved ivory tusks of the narwhal had long been a staple of the Greenland trade, and it has been suggested that in recent centuries Hanseatic merchants had protected their monopoly in this valuable product by obscuring its Arctic origins, substituting tales of mythical animals from vague eastern lands.

Engraving of a narwhal found by Frobisher's crew on a Baffin Island beach in 1577 (from Stefansson and McCaskill 1938; photo Harry Foster)

The frozen ocean was a source of both danger and pleasure, as it still is to any southerner. George Best, who left the most complete account of the Frobisher voyages, describes not only the dread inspired by icebergs and moving pack ice but the delight experienced by newcomers to the flat, landfast ice of early summer:

But now I remember I saw very strange wonders, men walking, running, leaping & floting upon the maine seas 40 miles from any land, without any Shippe or other vessell under them. Also I saw fresh Rivers running amidst the salt Sea a hundred myle from land, which if any man will not beleeve, let him know that many of our company lept out of their Shippe uppon Ilands of Ise, and running there uppe and downe, did shoote at buttes uppon the Ise, and with their Calivers did kill great Ceales, which use to lye and sleepe upon the Ise, and this Ise melting above at the toppe by reflection of the Sunne, came downe in sundrye streames, whyche uniting togither, made a prettie brooke able to drive a Mill. (Best's account of the 1578 voyage)

At times the English were oppressed by the heat of Arctic summer, and they were tempted to think of the environment as only slightly different from that of northern Europe. But the savagery of the Arctic winter seems to have been beyond their comprehension, and they had no compunction about planning to establish a winter settlement based on prefabricated and probably uninsulated wooden barracks. Before returning home in 1578, they even made an experimental planting of European crops on an Arctic island: "Also here we sowed pease, corne, and other graine, to prove the fruitfulnesse of the soyle against the next yeare" (Best's account of the 1578 voyage).

In cases such as this, the response of the English to Arctic conditions was that of people who sought the familiar in the alien, while at other times they expected to encounter matters and occurrences that were beyond the experience and understanding of their own world. This sense of entering a magical region, a vast and bleak version of Prospero's island, must have helped to stimulate expectations of fortune among the Elizabethan English who first penetrated this frozen realm.

Two

A Passage to Cathay

BY THE MIDDLE OF THE SIXTEENTH CENTURY the English were far behind their European neighbours in the race to establish trade and commercial outposts in distant regions of the world. For a century the Portuguese had pioneered sea routes down the western coast of Africa, discovering and exploiting new sources of gold, ivory, and slaves. Rounding the Cape of Good Hope, Portuguese caravels by AD 1500 had reached India and opened the spice trade from Southeast Asia. The Spanish, following the explorations of Christopher Columbus, had rapidly expanded their presence in the Caribbean and South America. With Hernando Cortés's conquest of Mexico in 1520 and Ferdinand Magellan's circumnavigation through the southern oceans two years later, Spain became the first European power to have significant commercial and military interests around the globe.

In sixteenth-century Europe the sovereignty of non-European lands was very much a religious matter. For centuries the Christian pope had been seen by Europeans not only as a spiritual ruler but as the ruler from whom temporal power descended to the sovereigns of Christian countries. In order to clarify the competing rights of Portugal and Spain, Alexander VI issued a papal bull in 1493 recognizing Portuguese claims to exploration, commerce, and conquest in the southern and eastern regions of the world and similar recognition for Spain in the New World discovered by Columbus. Ratified the following year by the Treaty of Tordesillas, the boundary between the two spheres was set as a longitudinal line about two thousand kilometres west of the Cape Verde Islands off the western coast of Africa. Since navigators of the time had no means of determining longitude, this boundary was very vaguely defined. In practice, however, it conceded to Portuguese interests some eastern portions of the New World: Brazil in the south and Newfoundland, Labrador, and Greenland in the north. From their mid-Atlantic base in the Azores, the Portuguese launched a series of northwestern explorations during the late fifteenth century, possibly discovering Newfoundland and certainly laying the basis for the major development of a Portuguese cod fishery in Newfoundland waters during succeeding centuries.

While Portugal and Spain developed wealth and power from their Asian and transatlantic enterprises, English sovereigns were slow to support the merchants and venturers who wished to undertake similar projects. John Cabot's attempt in 1497 to reach Asia by sailing directly westward from northern Europe won reluctant English support. He claimed his "Newe Found Islande," which he may have thought of as an outlier of the Asian continent, on behalf of the English king. However, succeeding exploration was limited to a few tentative westward probes, the earlier of which were organized in association with Azorean Portuguese interests. John Cabot's son Sebastian may have made an unsuccessful search for a northwestern passage to the East around 1508, but the official view of the time concluded that the voyage had occurred only in his imagination. Nothing came of a 1527 voyage organized by merchants of Bristol; one ship disappeared, while the other turned southwards after meeting icebergs in Newfoundland waters and continued to the Caribbean.

One reason for English lack of action may have been the papal bull of 1493 dividing the non-European world between Portugal and Spain, implicitly excluding other Christian rulers from enjoying full rights of discovery and exploitation. This impediment was removed when Henry VIII broke with the Roman church, but fear of a rupture with Spain may have prolonged England's lack of enthusiasm for overseas ventures. Even a half-century later, in describing Humphrey Gilbert's voyage to Newfoundland in 1583, Edward Hayes contrasted England's lack of activity with that of the French in the western Atlantic: "The French, as they can pretend less title unto these northern parts than the Spaniard, by how much the Spaniard made the first discovery of the same continent so far northward as unto Florida, and the French did but review that before discovered by the English nation, usurping upon our right, and imposing names upon countries, rivers, bays, capes, or headlands as if they had been the first finders of those coasts; which injury we offered not unto the Spaniards, but left off to discover when we approached the Spanish limits."

The French king, not to be excluded from the chance of distant riches, from the 1520s to 1540s had commissioned Giovanni da Verrazano, Jacques Cartier, and Jean-François de Roberval to explore the North American coasts and seek a westerly route to Asian wealth. France was at war with Spain for much of this period, which seems to have been sufficient reason for it to ignore the papal ruling that most of the New World was Spanish territory. By mid-century, French interests in North America had been confirmed, and fleets from Brittany and Normandy were major competitors of the Portuguese in the western Atlantic cod fishery. From the neighbouring Basque country, dozens of whaling ships arrived in Newfoundland and Labrador waters each summer, establishing shore stations where oil was rendered and poured into barrels for shipment to Europe. Some historians have estimated that the value of whale oil and salt codfish exported during the sixteenth century from what is now Atlantic Canada was equivalent to the value of precious metals extracted by the Spanish from Mexico and Peru during the same period. Yet, although Newfoundland had ostensibly been discovered by Cabot and claimed for England, very few English ships participated in this bonanza during the first half of the sixteenth century.

The accession of Queen Mary in 1553, together with the restoration of Catholicism as England's official religion and the renewal of political alliance with Spain, may have been influential in directing English exploration in a new direction — northwards into regions where neither the Spanish nor the Portuguese had shown interest. The era of English Arctic exploration began in that year with the first attempt by English merchants to reach Asia using a sea route to the north of Norway. This voyage ended with the death from cold and starvation of Hugh Willoughby and the crews of two ships on the frozen coasts of the Barents Sea. A third ship, under the pilot Richard Chancellor, succeeded in rounding the Kola Peninsula and reached the Russian coast near the present-day city of Archangel, from where Chancellor travelled overland to the Moscow of Ivan the Terrible and opened a profitable trade with the Russian kingdom.

The Company of Merchant Adventurers, which had been originally chartered in 1551, now changed its name to the Muscovy Company, and the search for a Northeast Passage to Asia was combined with trading voyages along Europe's Arctic coast as well as overland through what is now southern Russia. English and Dutch navigators eventually reached the mouth of the Ob River, but their ventures were tales of suffering, loss, and defeat to the ice-choked waters off the northern Siberian coast. When the Cossack Semyon Dezhnev reached the Bering Strait in 1648, it was not by ship but by a combination of overland and coastal travel using small river boats.

Queen Elizabeth I was crowned in 1558, and the new monarch re-established the Church of England and began to allow new policies towards Spain. Although England and Spain remained at peace, English privateers soon began to encroach on Spanish commerce in the Caribbean, and international politics became less of an impediment to English exploration. In the north the first decade of Elizabeth's reign coincided with the growing suspicion that a Northeast Passage to Asia would be difficult to discover and probably impossible to develop for commercial navigation. English eyes began to turn to the west, where Spanish interests were now of less concern and where early-sixteenth-century hopes of a through passage to Asia had soon flagged after Cabot and his successors had encountered only the ice-strewn waters and bleak coasts of Newfoundland, Labrador, and Greenland.

The concept of a Northwest Passage, an Arctic route to Asia that would be shorter and less arduous than the immensely long course through the southern oceans used by Spain and Portugal, flourished in England during the 1560s and 1570s. Three figures were central to this development, epitomizing the three vocations that converged to produce the dynamic character of Elizabethan enterprise: Sir Humphrey Gilbert, soldier and promoter of grand schemes; John Dee, scientist and mystic; and Michael Lok, merchant and backer of commercial ventures. Even in an age that produced figures whose capacities and endeavours seem larger and more brilliant than those of the present century, these men were conspicuous by the breadth of their interests, talents, and accomplishments. All three were vital to the enterprise that eventually placed Martin Frobisher in Arctic Canada and initiated an English claim to northern North America.

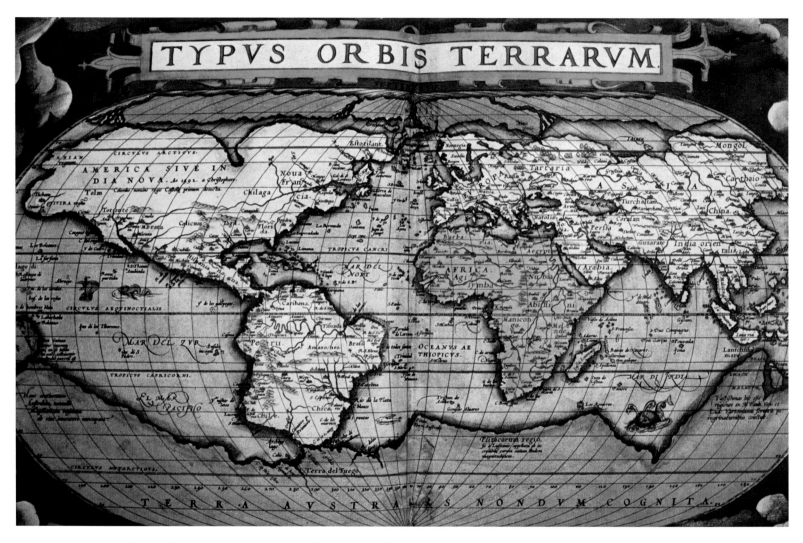

The world map drawn in 1570 by the Flemish geographer Abraham Ortelius shows an assumed Northwest Passage through Arctic North America (courtesy Bernard Allaire; photo Harry Foster).

Sir Humphrey Gilbert, Soldier and Promoter

Humphrey Gilbert, the elder half-brother of Sir Walter Raleigh, was born in 1539 to a landowning family with property near the English West Country port of Dartmouth. He does not seem to have enjoyed his Oxford education, an experience that led him later in life to design and propose a new university curriculum which would be of greater use and relevance in the education of a gentleman. By the age of twenty he was a hanger-on at the court of Elizabeth, and at twenty-four he received a military commission from her. Over the following decade Gilbert distinguished himself as a valiant soldier in the religious wars being fought on the continent, as well as in the brutal suppression of rebellion in Ireland. His later interest in establishing an English colony in America may have arisen from his part in settling English communities in Ulster, a project for "civilizing" the native Irish population that resonates to the present day. In the intervals between military assignments, Gilbert interested himself in advancing the fortunes of England, and his own, by developing a scheme for discovering and exploiting a new route to Asia. In 1566 he wrote a lengthy pamphlet entitled *A Discourse of a Discoverie for a New Passage to Cataia*. It was not published until a decade later in association with the Frobisher project, but it seems to have been influential before that time.

The *Discourse* is a fascinating assemblage of the curious geographical and historical knowledge of the time, combined with arguments from "authority" and "reason" that are quite alien to the modern mind. Gilbert begins his discourse by stating his purpose: to prove that the American continents are bounded on the north by "the sea that severeth it from Grondland, thorow which Northern seas, the passage lyeth, which I take now in hande to discover." His "arguments from authority" begin with that of Plato, who stated that Atlantis was an immense island in the western ocean. Since no large islands remain to be discovered, Atlantis must be identified with America; therefore America is an island with sea to the north as well as to east, west, and south. Other ancient writers and contemporary mapmakers are also called as authorities on the existence of open sea to the north of America. Gilbert's "arguments from reason" are based on the mistaken belief that the northward-flowing Gulf Stream derives from waters rushing westward around the Cape of Good Hope, and that they must have a northwesterly outlet in order to replenish the waters of the Indian Ocean. This view is combined with the reasonable argument that if America was joined to Asia, it would have been penetrated by Tartars, Scythians, and other Asiatic peoples and animals, none of which have been encountered in New Spain or Newfoundland. Gilbert next summarizes several vague accounts of travellers who claimed to have reached or traversed a Northwest Passage, most notably Sebastian Cabot, who said that he had been cheerfully sailing northwards in open water above the Arctic Circle when he was forced to turn back by a mutiny of his sailors. Gilbert then turns to accounts, beginning with the Roman historian Pliny and continuing to the twelfth century AD, of strange men being cast up by the sea on the coasts of Europe, and contends by complex and unconvincing arguments that these must have been Asians who had passed across the northern edge of the American continents before being driven onto Europe.

Having satisfied himself that a navigable sea passage exists to the north of America, Gilbert lists the benefits that its discovery would bring to England. The English would gain access to the Asian trade now monopolized by Spain and Portugal, "which would be a great advancement to our Countrie, wonderfull inriching to our prince, and unspeakable commodities to all the inhabitants of Europe." They would also be able to reach yet-undiscovered Eastern lands, "where ther is to be found great aboundance of gold, silver, precious stones, Cloth of golde, silkes, all maner of Spices, Grocery wares, and other kinds of Merchandize, of an inestimable price: which both the Spaniarde and Portingal, through the length of their journeys, can not well attaine unto." These newly discovered countries would also provide a market for English cloth, the export of which was a staple of commercial activity at the time, and the trade would result in an increase in the English fleet without burdening the treasury. Finally, the establishment of English settlement along the shores of the Passage and in newly discovered lands would serve as an outlet for "suche needie people of our Countrie, which now trouble the common welth, and through want here at home, are inforced to commit outragious offences, whereby they are dayly consumed with the Gallowes." Importantly, England could develop these benefits "without injurie done to any Christian prince, by crossing them in any of their used trades, whereby they might take any just occasion of offence."

Gilbert closes his pamphlet with an encouraging comparison between his geographical knowledge and that of Columbus, and he boasts that he has developed a means "for the perfect knowing of the longitude" as well as "infallible rules" for determining whether an inlet is merely a bay or in fact a through passage to another sea. He concludes with the proclamation "That he is not worthie to live at all, that for feare, or daunger of death, shunneth his countrey service, and his owne honour, seeing death is inevitable, and the fame of vertue immortell." Martin Frobisher, in undertaking the discovery of the Northwest Passage, would certainly have agreed with this sentiment. However, his undertaking would have been far simpler and more successful had Gilbert's "perfect knowing" and "infallible rules" of navigation been more than the boasts or self-delusions of a man who is seen by history as one of the greatest promoters in Elizabethan England.

JOHN DEE, SCIENTIST AND MYSTIC

The second figure whose interests and knowledge were central to the Frobisher venture was John Dee, considered the most learned man in Europe during the latter part of the sixteenth century. Humphrey Gilbert noted in his introduction to the *Discourse of a Discoverie for a New Passage to Cataia* that "a great learned man (even M. Dee) doth seeme very well to like of this Discoverie, and doth much commende the Authour, the which he declareth in his Mathematical preface to the english Euclid."

Born in London in 1527, Dee came from a Welsh family that claimed a distant connection to the Tudors and had held a position at the court of Henry VIII. In 1542 he enrolled at Cambridge University, where he enthusiastically studied mathematics and ancient languages. His experience of university was quite different from that of Gilbert, and Dee writes of these years that "I did inviolably keepe this order; only to sleepe four houres every night; to allow to meate and drink (and some refreshing after) two houres every day; and of the other eighteen houres all (except the time of going to and being at divine service) was spent in my studies and learning." He also distinguished himself by designing a theatrical effect by which a man rose to the top of Trinity Hall, and which for the first time attracted charges of conjuring and associating with evil spirits. At the age of twenty Dee travelled to the Low Countries, where he met Gerhard Mercator and acquired from him two geographical globes and certain newly invented astronomical instruments, which he brought back to England. He received an MA the following year and then returned to Louvain to study with Mercator and the geographer and cosmographer Gemma Frisius. Continental Europe was at this time far in advance of England in geographical knowledge, as well as in astronomical learning and the associated techniques of navigation. During the following decades, Dee was at the forefront in introducing to England the techniques and instruments that had been developed on the continent, and he was generous in putting his knowledge at the disposal of those seeking to expand English influence into the remote regions of the world.

Dee's reputation for great learning developed from a series of lectures that he gave in 1550 at the University of Paris, where "for the honour of my country I did undertake to read freely and publiquely Euclide's Elements Geometricall, Mathematice Physice et Pythagorice; a thing never done publiquely in any University of Christendome." Refusing European offers of patronage, he returned to England in 1551 and entered the employ of Edward VI. The first evidence of Dee's involvement in exploration comes two years later, when he composed *Astronomicall and logisticall rules and Canons, to calculate the Ephemerides by, and other necessary accounts of heavenly motions: written at the request, and for the use of that excellent Mechanicien Master Richard Chauncelor, at his last voyage into Moschovia.* Chancellor, we may recall, was the leading figure in the Muscovy Company who in 1553 had made a successful voyage through the Barents Sea to Archangel and thus overland to Moscow.

The accession of Queen Mary inaugurated a dangerous time for scholars, and in 1555 Dee was arrested and examined on charges "that I endeavoured by enchantments to destroy Queene Mary." These charges seem to have arisen from horoscopes that he had cast for the future Queen Elizabeth, and Dee was cleared and released only after a rigorous investigation of his political and religious beliefs. His fortunes changed when Elizabeth came to power in 1558, and in fact he was commissioned to prepare an astrological prediction for her coronation date. For the next quarter-century Dee remained close to the centre of English power, patronized by the court and charged with numerous and varied intellectual tasks. He published widely but obscurely, and most of his writings have long since been lost. His lectures and publications over this period established his reputation as the leading scholar of the day. Dee also assembled a library of over four thousand volumes, which may have been the most complete library in Europe, together with laboratories "replenished with chemical stuff (for above twenty years) of my getting together far and neare, with great paines, costs and dangers." Elizabeth herself visited his house at Mortlake, in order to view the celebrated library and meet with her private astrologer, philosopher, and mage.

Science and learning were undergoing rapid change in northern Europe during the mid-sixteenth century. The Renaissance, which had begun a century or more earlier in southern Europe, was now beginning to significantly influence the countries of the north, stimulating a fundamental change from medieval to modern modes of thinking about the world and its meaning. The philosophy and science that John Dee learned and practised was a curious amalgamation of the old and newer ways of thought: astrology was intimately linked to an astronomy that postulated new and rational means of investigating the movements of heavenly bodies; practical chemistry was being developed for the assaying of metals and the production of materials, yet chemical processes were explained in terms of alchemical principles; mathematics was newly linked with the recently rediscovered cabbalistic tradition of Jewish learning, and the solutions to practical problems were investigated at the same time as mathematicians searched for numerological insights into the structure of the universe. Dee, as can be seen from the events of his later life, seems to have possessed more than the usual scholarly interest in the mystical aspects of learning. His portrait shows an impressively long-bearded elder in rich dress, the perfect image of a late-medieval wizard.

Throughout the 1560s and 1570s, John Dee was associated with the Muscovy Company and acted as adviser and consultant to many of those exploring distant regions. By the 1570s he was engaged in writing a series of volumes titled *General and Rare Memorials Pertayning to the Perfect Art of Navigation*. He had invented two new instruments that he called the "Paradoxall Compass" and the "Compass of Variation."

Portrait of the scholar and
mystic John Dee by an
unknown artist (Ashmolean
Museum, Oxford)

The latter seems to have been designed to measure the extent of magnetic variation
from true north, a phenomenon which is caused by the fact that the needle of the
magnetic compass does not point to the geographical North Pole but to the North
Magnetic Pole, which is not stable but has wandered widely over much of Arctic
Canada during the past few centuries. In Dee's time the Magnetic Pole was thought
of as a fixed location, and it appears on Mercator's 1569 map as a huge mountain of
iron. On this assumption Dee's Compass of Variation may have led him to believe,
as he stated in 1576, that he had developed a method of determining longitude.
Humphrey Gilbert made the same assertion in his *Discourse*, published the same year,
in which he claimed support from Dee. The error of supposing a solution to the
longitude problem may have originated with Dee and have only been appropriated
by Gilbert.

In the early summer of 1576 Dee was asked to instruct Frobisher and his navigator, Christopher Hall, in the skills of navigating in northern latitudes. He advised them on the purchase of maps, books, and navigational instruments and gave them a short but intensive course in the mathematical basis of navigation. Dee feared that insufficient time had been allowed to teach them properly, and indeed, it is likely that the seamen understood little of what they were taught. They certainly did not learn how to determine longitude, nor did they successfully master Gilbert's "infallible" methods of distinguishing a bay from a strait or passage.

John Dee's broad interests encompassed another field that was of subsequent relevance to the Frobisher venture. During the 1570s and early 1580s he developed a growing concern for the advance of England's place in the world. The voyages in search of the Northwest Passage were valued primarily for the claims that they established on newly discovered lands, and after the Frobisher voyages Dee prepared at the Queen's request a map and charter detailing her historic rights to possession of the northern portions of America (this document is described in a later chapter). He is credited with inventing the concept of the British Empire and with setting out the legal basis for such an institution. Dee also had a personal interest in English expansion, for in 1580, in return for advice similar to that supplied to the Frobisher party, he was able to record that "Sir Humfrey Gilbert graunted me my request to him made by letter, for the royalties of discovery all to the north above the parallell of the 50 degree of latitude."

For a few years, therefore, John Dee was the theoretical owner of the greater part of the territory that now makes up Canada. However, the title seems to have lapsed in 1583, when Humphrey Gilbert drowned while returning from establishing an English claim to Newfoundland. The same year Dee left England for Europe in company with the alchemist and medium Edward Kelly, with whom he would be associated in spiritualist activities for several years. When he finally returned to England in 1589, impoverished and perhaps disillusioned with mystical knowledge, he found that his library had been destroyed by a mob and his reputation as a respected scholar and statesman replaced by that of a feared conjurer and practitioner of black magic.

MICHAEL LOK, MERCHANT VENTURER

While Humphrey Gilbert provided the visionary energy and the royal connections required to organize a project to discover a Northwest Passage, and John Dee supplied the geographical and navigational knowledge that made such a scheme seem plausible, the financial backing for the enterprise was centred on a third figure, Michael Lok. He was descended from at least three generations of London merchants who had been closely associated with the Mercers Company, the guild that dealt in the export of English cloth. Lok's father had risen to become one of the leading merchants in England, as well as an ardent supporter of Henry VIII and the Protestant cause. His older half-brother, Thomas, was a founding member of the Muscovy Company and had backed the voyage taken by Willoughby and Chancellor in 1553. The following year he organized a trading expedition to the West African coast, a venture that left the teenaged Martin Frobisher a hostage of the Portuguese.

Michael Lok was born in 1532 and spent much of his early life out of England, involved in various aspects of the family business. After a five-year teenage apprenticeship in the Low Countries, he worked in Spain and Portugal between 1552 and 1556, before moving to Venice and serving in the valuable trade to the eastern Mediterranean for three years. This lengthy sojourn abroad probably had political as well as business motives, since they spanned the reign of Queen Mary, during which various members of the prominently Protestant Lok family suffered imprisonment and exile. Queen Elizabeth's accession brought Michael back to England in 1559. There the diverse knowledge and contacts that he had gained during his sojourn in Europe must have served to advance the family's business. He married the daughter of the sheriff of London, who brought to the marriage considerable wealth and social connections. Lok appears to have set about his business with energy and originality, as witness a proposal that he presented unsuccessfully to the Privy Council for the development of a silk-manufacturing industry in England.

By the end of the 1560s Lok had accumulated considerable wealth, though he left few records of his activities and accomplishments. In 1571 he was appointed London agent for the Muscovy Company, a position that placed him at the centre of the ventures in northern exploration. It was in this capacity that in 1574 he met Martin Frobisher, an acquaintanceship that was to have devastating consequences for him. By this time Lok had fifteen children and stepchildren. He was now head of the family enterprises founded by his great-grandfather and had attained a solid and assured position in the English merchant community. James McDermott, who has recently written the most complete account of Michael Lok's career, notes that "had he continued to nurture his business in the prudent manner which appears to have characterized the first, relatively anonymous half of his mature life, Michael Lok might well have enjoyed his remaining years in a comfort denied to all but a few members of the contemporary non-aristocratic population. Unfortunately, his nature could not allow such relative contentment to remain undisturbed."

The first proposal for a Northwest Passage venture, which Frobisher submitted to the Muscovy Company in late 1574, was turned down. Lok was a member of the committee that assessed and rejected this proposal, yet by the following spring he had changed his mind and joined Frobisher to request a licence for such an enterprise. Over the next three years Lok's efforts were crucial in securing ever-increasing investments for the operation and assembling a company of wealthy and influential backers. As well, he invested heavily on his own account in order to cover any shortfalls. The reasons for his enthusiasm, energy, and commitment to the project remain unclear. He did not lack wealth or recognition, yet he invested far more in money and reputation than anyone else involved in the venture, and when it ended, he suffered more than any of his associates. The Frobisher voyages would bankrupt Michael Lok; he would be imprisoned several times as a result of the debts that he accumulated; and as late as 1615, at the age of eighty-three, he was still being sued by the estates of people whose backing he had obtained.

Lok himself seems to have been puzzled by this turn that his life had taken. Looking back on this period, he wrote,

Yf I had followed my vocation onely, and had attended on myne owne ordinary busynes, as other Marchanttes doo and as my fryndes often have parswaded with me, And had not spent my tyme, my Labour, & my money, in these strainge matters of the Common-welthe, thes many yeres, I myght have gotten and kept x^{iii}. Li. [£10,000] of money, as others have done, but God who is the director of all mens welldoynge, hath styll drawen my mynd, and as it were forced me (notwithstandynge my often repugnance, through feare of Lak of Mayntaynance for my great famylye to the study of the matter) for summ good purpose, unknown to me.

Today Michael Lok's name is mainly encountered in connection with two rather dubious memorials. One is Loks Land, the barren Arctic island named by Frobisher which marks the northern entrance to Frobisher Bay and has long been avoided by the Inuit of the area as a place of great misfortune. The other is in the small literary industry maintained by those who believe that Shakespeare's plays were not written by "the man from Stratford" but by Edward de Vere, 17th Earl of Oxford. Lok persuaded the earl to gamble heavily on the final Frobisher expedition. The loss of the earl's money and his resulting debt to Lok is, according to these theorists, memorialized in the name of the despised moneylender Shylock in *The Merchant of Venice*.

Three

MARTIN FROBISHER, PIRATE AND EXPLORER

MARTIN FROBISHER EMERGES FROM THE SHADOWS of history through his role in two great events. The first, his involvement in the voyages in search of the Northwest Passage in 1576–78, ended in failure and condemnation. By contrast, his part in the naval defence against the Spanish Armada in 1588 was rewarded with celebrity and a knighthood. He passed the rest of his career in relative obscurity, the hard lot of a mariner who had no great distinction of family or wealth and who depended on his skill and character to survive in a world where relatives and affluence were essential to advancement.

The obscurity begins with his birth. Even the family name is a mystery, "Frobisher" being merely a standardized spelling agreeed on by historians. Members of the family at the time variously signed the name Furbisher, Furbiser, Ffourbyssher, Ffurbussher, Froobiser, and doubtless other ways as well. Nor do we know the date of his birth. When testifying against charges of piracy in 1566, he gave his age as twenty-seven, which would place his date of birth as 1538 or 1539. However, other evidence suggests that 1535 or 1536 is more likely. Frobisher himself may not have been certain of his own age.

Frobisher's birthplace is known, however: the farm of Altofts, in the interior dales of Yorkshire in northern England, an unlikely locality to produce a great mariner. His family had some local prominence, his uncle being mayor of the nearby town of Doncaster in 1535 and his mother the daughter of a local knight. His father died when Martin was about ten years old, and his mother three years later. The orphaned and probably impoverished boy was sent to live with relatives of his mother, the family of the London merchant Sir John York. Here the accidents of

Portrait of Martin Frobisher
by Cornelius Ketel, 1577 (Bodleian
Library, Oxford)

family placed him in a position to take up his future calling.

We know nothing of Frobisher's education, and it seems to have been minimal. Those who have attempted to decipher his handwriting uniformly remark on its illegibility; and even in an age when consistency in spelling was not a prized virtue, Frobisher's was more idiosyncratic than most. In view of his apparent lack of aptitude for schooling, combined with the quick temper and impatience that characterized the man in later life, it is perhaps not surprising that his guardian found an early opportunity to place him on board a ship sailing for an exotic destination. As his biographer William McFee writes, "He was sent to sea because they could do nothing with him ashore. At sea he remained for forty years, with scarcely any rest, and in action he died."

Young Frobisher's first nautical experience was memorable and almost fatal. In 1553, at about the age of seventeen, he shipped with the first English expedition to trespass on the traditional West African territory of the Portuguese. The venture comprised three ships and 140 men under Thomas Wyndham, and it returned with a fortune in gold, and pepper, which was paid for with the deaths by heat or disease of over two-thirds of the crew, including Wyndham himself. The experience did not discourage Frobisher, who sailed for West Africa the following year on a similar expedition, this one financed by Thomas Lok and under the command of John Lok, older brothers of Michael Lok. While trading at a location on the West African coast, Frobisher volunteered to go ashore as a hostage. According to Richard Hakluyt's account, "the Captaine thereof would needs have a pledge ashore. But when they received the pledge, they kept him still, and would trafficke no more, but shot off their ordinance at us." The hostage was abandoned by the expedition, which went elsewhere to trade and eventually returned to England with a rich cargo of gold, pepper and elephant ivory, but without Martin Frobisher.

Nothing more was heard of Frobisher until he arrived in England three or four years later. It is assumed that the Africans who captured him turned him over to the local Portuguese, who imprisoned him for eight months in their fortress at Mina in Guinea. From here he was somehow transferred to Lisbon and eventually repatriated to England. It was a stunning adventure for a young man who, a decade before, had not yet left the Yorkshire dales. By about the age of twenty-three Frobisher had experienced dangers and cultural shocks beyond the imagination of most Englishmen and been in contact with Iberian mariners whose knowledge and experience of distant oceans was unsurpassed. His African adventures gave an education much different from that of other young Englishmen at the time, and it provided him with the foundation for the skills and character on which he built his subsequent career.

Returning to England at about the same time that Queen Elizabeth came to the throne, Martin Frobisher found new opportunities open to a young mariner with experience of distant seas and hazardous journeys. The new queen's break with the Catholic Church and the termination of England's previous political alliance with Spain opened the way to new markets for trade and new targets for military and commercial enterprises. Privateering was recognized as a commercial activity closely allied with the country's political aims, and licences were issued to mariners who were willing to risk their lives and ships to seize cargoes belonging to French Catholics or other groups not allied with the English in the religious wars that consumed Europe at the time.

Frobisher soon found himself in the privateering business. It has been suggested that his first voyage may have been planned as a raiding or slaving venture to the Guinea coast that would make use of the local knowledge he had gained during his recent captivity there, but such a plan does not seem to have been carried out. By 1563 Frobisher was in charge of a ship owned and licensed by his brother John, supposedly preying on French merchant ships. However, Martin's part in the illegal despoiling of the Spanish ship *Katherine* led to his being jailed on the first of several occasions. Two years later he was free and the owner of two ships, perhaps purchased with his illegal gains of 1563. Frobisher next appears on a list of complaints made by the Spanish ambassador to England, charged with the plundering in 1565 of the Andalusian ship *Flying Spirit*. A year later he was arrested once again while apparently preparing for an illegal voyage to Guinea, perhaps involving slaving or raids on Portuguese establishments, but he was soon released. Frobisher seems to have stayed free of the law for the following two years, but in 1569 the merchants of the English Channel port of Rye complained of his activities to the Privy Council.

He was sued for seizing a cargo of wine shipped by a London merchant aboard a French Protestant ship and was eventually arrested for the illegal capture of another French ship. This time his reputation for continual breaches of the fine line between legal privateering and illegal piracy seems to have been cause for a more serious sentence than the fines and brief imprisonments that he had received for previous infractions. The episode brought an end to the piratical phase of Frobisher's career, and when we hear of him again two years later, he is in command of a ship outfitted by the Queen.

The transformation of Martin Frobisher from pirate to naval officer remains a mystery. It may have been due to the intervention of merchant acquaintances to whom he turned for help during his imprisonment. Records indicate that an associate sold Frobisher's ship, perhaps without payment, to Lady Elizabeth Clinton, who was wife of the lord high admiral and a friend of the Queen. In return, the Queen and the Privy Council may have been made aware of the plight of a skilled mariner and competent leader, proven in hazardous circumstances and useful for dangerous undertakings. After his release from prison, Frobisher's first commission was to sail against smugglers and privateers, who were temporarily being suppressed by the Crown. In 1572 he was sent to Ireland, where Humphrey Gilbert was in command of troops putting down a rebellion.

Aside from an isolated charge of piracy for which he was never arrested, we know little of Frobisher's activities over the next three years. However, the incomplete records of the time hint at his involvement in three discrete episodes that might be considered treasonous. In 1572 he was approached by the Earl of Desmond, an Irish aristocrat who was being held hostage in London, and he may have accepted a large sum to smuggle the earl and his family to Ireland before the plot was betrayed and the earl arrested. The following year Frobisher was offered money to carry English Catholic agents to Spain, where they hoped to raise an army to invade Ireland, and his ship was arrested by order of the Privy Council. In 1575 the Spanish ambassador in London approached him with the offer of an undertaking on behalf of the king of Spain and understood that he had accepted the overture. The fact that Frobisher escaped recorded punishment for any of these episodes has led his biographers to suggest that he was serving England as an *agent provocateur* or that he had loyally betrayed each of the schemes to the Queen or council. On the other hand, the fact that he continued to be considered a potential traitor by England's enemies suggests that his reputation, and perhaps his record were not entirely clear.

The same historical clouds that obscure our view of Frobisher's public life as privateer and explorer almost totally hide the private and family life of the man. Orphaned in his early teens, he may have had few later contacts with his immediate family. We know only that he undertook privateering ventures with a brother during the 1560s and that he later provided for his brothers' children. He married twice while in his forties and fifties, on both occasions to wealthy older widows whose fortunes found good use in his projects. Isabel Frobisher, whom he married in 1576 or 1577, was apparently destitute by the time her husband sailed on his third Arctic voyage in 1578. In a plaintive letter written to Secretary of State Sir Francis Walsingham during Frobisher's absence, she asked the Privy Council for relief: "your humble oratrix Isabell Frobusher, the most miserable poor woman in the world that whereas your honour's said oratrix sometimes was the wife of one Thomas Riggatt of Snathe in the County of York, a very wealthy man, who left your oratrix well to live and in very good state and good portions unto all his children. Afterwards she took to husband Mr. Captain Frobusher (whom God forgive) who hath not only spent that which her said husband left her, but the portions also of her poor children, and hath put them all to the wide world to shift a most lamentable case." We hear no more of Isabel, and in the early 1590s Frobisher married the wealthy widow Dorothy Widmerpool. We may fairly presume that his interests in marriage were primarily financial, and to our knowledge he left no children.

By 1575 Martin Frobisher, forty-year-old ex-pirate and potential sympathizer with the Irish and Spanish causes, would seem to have been an unlikely individual to be entrusted with a major English expedition in search of a new route to Asia. How he obtained such a position is one of the mysteries about the adventure that have not been solved. By his own account, he had been interested in the Northwest Passage for the previous twenty years. According to a pamphlet written by Richard Willes in support of the first Northwest Passage expedition, "We do read againe of a Portugal that passed this streite, of whom M. Furbisher speaketh, that was imprisoned therefore many yeeres in *Lesbona*, to verifie the olde Spanyshe proverbe, I suffer for doyng wel." Frobisher's interest may therefore have been sparked during his prison stay in Lisbon, by a chance meeting with an ancient mariner who claimed to have sailed from Pacific to Atlantic across the northern end of America. It is also possible that he had encountered Humphrey Gilbert during his service in Ireland and had been stimulated by that colonial promoter's enthusiasm for a Northwest Passage.

George Best also reports that Frobisher had long considered such a venture, had conferred with friends, and had finally devised a plan for its accomplishment, "knowing this to be the onely thing of the Worlde that was left undone, whereby a notable mind mighte be made famous and fortunate." In his edited version of Best's account, Vilhjalmur Stefansson cannot help adding the note, "To this day polar explorers are constantly announcing that what they plan to do, or have just returned from doing, is the last great task of discovery." The statement does seem particularly high-minded for a mariner of Frobisher's qualities and reputation, but we should not discount the possibility that, for whatever purpose, he had considered an expedition in search of the Northwest Passage for some time before acting on the idea.

By the mid-1570s, with the privateering business in decline, Frobisher may well have decided that the time was appropriate to turn his hand to other interests. He may have first approached acquaintances at court. There he could have caught the attention of Ambrose Dudley, Earl of Warwick, who later became an enthusiastic promoter of the venture. However, the obvious starting point for organizing an Arctic expedition was the Muscovy Company, the group of London merchants who for the past two decades had organized the various explorations for a Northeast Passage, developed trade with Russia, and held a licensed monopoly on northern ventures. Frobisher may have initially approached the company with a proposal from his friends at court. On the other hand, his access to the Muscovy Company may have been through its London agent, Michael Lok, whose brother had abandoned the young Frobisher on the coast of Guinea twenty years before. Lok's business term in Lisbon during 1555 and 1556 may have coincided with Frobisher's prison sojourn in that city, and it is even possible that Lok was involved in Frobisher's repatriation from Africa to a Portuguese prison and eventually to England. His account of the background to the Northwest Passage expeditions emphasizes his central role in the development of the venture, but he acknowledges that the first approach was made by Frobisher. Lok reminisced in a memoir that he had renewed an old acquaintance with the adventurer in 1574 and that "fynding him sufficient and ready to execute the attemp of so great matters, I joyned with him, and to my power advanced him to the world with credit and above myne own power for my parte furnished him with things necessary for his furst voyage lately made to the northwestward for the discovery of Cathay and other new cuntries, to thintent the whole world might be opened unto England which hitherto hath byn hydden from yt by the slowthfulness of some and policy of others"

For Martin Frobisher, a new phase of life had begun. In the words of his biographer William McFee, "The tide was on the turn. Martin Frobisher, sometime slaver and pirate of the Narrow Seas, had his foot on the first rung of the ladder which led to admiralty and a famous name in sea-history." The expectation of fortune, reputation, and adventure that fuelled his involvement in this career is well expressed in the only poem we know Frobisher to have written, which was published in 1583 in support of Gilbert's colonizing venture to Newfoundland:

A pleasant ayre, a sweete and firtell soile,
A certain gaine, a never dying praise:
An easie passage, voide of loathsome toile,
Found out by some, and knowen to me the waies.
All this is there, then who will refraine to trie:
That loves to live abroad, or dreades to die.

Four

TO ARCTIC AMERICA

FROM LATE 1574, WHEN MARTIN FROBISHER first presented his proposal to the Muscovy Company, until the summer of 1576, when he finally sailed for the Arctic regions, he and Michael Lok worked as a promotional team. Lok had considerable experience in organizing expeditions, but more importantly, he was acquainted with the people in the merchant community and at court whose approval was necessary if the venturers were to raise the funding and acquire the licences that would allow the enterprise to proceed. For his part, Frobisher provided the reputation of a mariner who had been proven in hardship and hazard, and was considered capable of carrying out a risky venture to the profit of all concerned. Together they obtained from the Muscovy Company a licence to undertake northern exploration, and they began to assemble financial backers. The voyage was originally planned for the summer of 1575, but the money collected was insufficient and the time too short for the newly formed association to organize such a complicated enterprise, and the expedition was delayed until the following year.

The setback gave the venturers time to canvass more broadly for financial backing and advice, which they clearly needed. Their effort must have been significantly advanced by the publication of Humphrey Gilbert's *A Discourse of a Discoverie for a New Passage to Cataia*, originally written ten years earlier but not printed until April 1576. The publisher noted that interest in the *Discourse* was stimulated "because I understoode that M. Fourboiser (a kinsman of mine) did pretend to travaile in the same Discoverie," and it is clear that the pamphlet was published at this time in order to raise interest in the enterprise. However, we may suspect that the timely publication was also designed to stake Gilbert's claim to the idea of a profitable

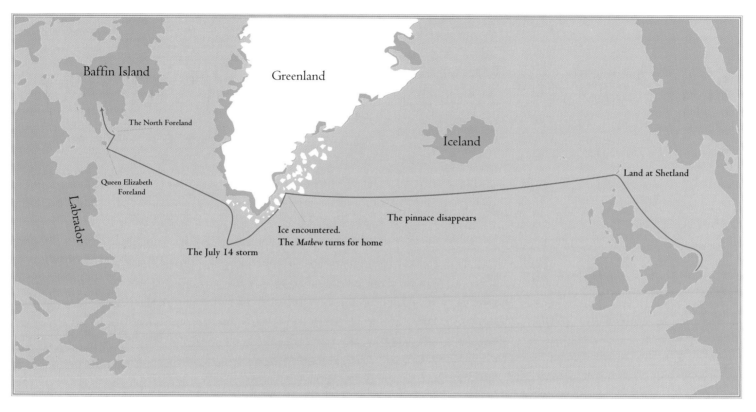

Baffin Island

Greenland

The North Foreland

Iceland

Queen Elizabeth
Foreland

Land at Shetland

Labrador

The pinnace disappears

Ice encountered.
The *Mathew* turns for home

The July 14 storm

Northwest Passage. Lok's reaction suggests the latter interpretation, since he wrote, "Although to say the very truthe without geving any offence: neither that boke comming out so late nor yet his former discourses, being none others than were well known to us long before, were any manner of causes or instructions to the chief enterprises of this new voyage of discovery to attempt the same or to direct us therin." That is to say, there was nothing new here that was not common knowledge, and plans for the voyage were already in place before the pamphlet was published.

Lok was not averse to taking advice, however, and he invited the scholar John Dee to his house, together with several of the leading navigators in the Muscovy trade, in order to discuss the route of the expedition and recommend the books, maps, and navigational instruments that would be needed on the voyage. As we have seen,

The northern world, showing Frobisher's 1576 route to Arctic Canada

Dee put considerable effort into training Frobisher and his navigator, Christopher Hall, in mathematical and navigational techniques. Lok eventually assembled a group of eighteen investors drawn from both the merchants of London and officials of the court, who ventured a total of £875; he himself made up the extra £738 that was required, in addition to his original investment of £100.

After an unsuccessful attempt to fund the construction of a large ship, a fleet of three small vessels was assembled. The *Gabriel*, of about thirty tons burden, was built for the expedition, and a somewhat smaller ship, the *Michael*, was purchased for £120. The third vessel was a tiny pinnace, less than half the size of the others, which was to be used in coastal exploration of shallow waters. Even the two barks, *Gabriel* and *Michael*, were miniscule by the standards of the day, about half the size of the smallest of Columbus's fleet of almost a century before or of the *Mathew*, which carried Cabot on his voyage to Newfoundland in 1497. The *Gabriel* and the *Michael* were about the size of the Norse *knorrs*

A TRVE DISCOVRSE of the late voyages of difcouerie, for the finding of a paffage to Cathaya, by the Northvveaft, vnder the conduct of *Martin Frobifher* Generall: Deuided into three Bookes.

In the firft wherof is fhewed, his firft voyage. Wherein alfo by the vvay is fette out a Geographicall defcription of the Worlde, and what partes therof haue bin difcouered by the Nauigations of the Englifhmen.

Alfo, there are annexed certayne reafons, to proue all partes of the Worlde habitable, with a generall Mappe adioyned.

In the fecond, is fet out his fecond voyage, vvith the aduentures and accidents thereof.

In the thirde, is declared the ftrange fortunes which hapned in the third voyage, with a feuerall defcription of the Countrey and the people there inhabiting. VVith a particular Card therevnto adioyned of *Meta Incognita*, fo farre forth as the fecretes of the voyage may permit.

AT LONDON, Imprinted by Henry Bynnyman, feruant to the right Honourable Sir CHRISTOPHER HATTON Vizchamberlaine. *Anno Domini*.1578.

Title page of George Best's 1578 report on the three Frobisher voyages, the most complete of several published accounts (from Stefansson and McCaskill 1938; photo Harry Foster)

that had plied the seas between Europe and Greenland for the previous five centuries, although with their full decks and more complex rigging, they were more seaworthy. They would have been three-masted vessels, probably about fifteen metres long overall and with a beam of only about four metres, smaller and more fragile than many of the private yachts that today make transatlantic crossings. The small size of the vessels may have been chosen because they would be navigating ice and the narrow channels that might lead to a western sea, but it seems as likely that the choice was forced on the consortium by the limited funds available. Money was found, however, to carve a dragon figurehead for the *Gabriel*.

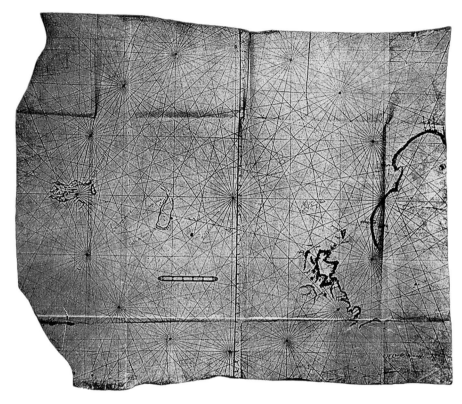

The chart used by Frobisher when he crossed the North Atlantic in 1576 (from Stefansson and McCaskill 1938; photo Harry Foster)

Expense was not spared on books, maps, and navigational instruments. Thanks to Michael Lok's detailed accounting practices, we have a rare record of the equipment and supplies that were purchased for the expedition. The books included the *Cosmographie universelle* (in French), published the previous year by André Thevet; a large English Bible; both English- and French-language versions of Thevet's volume on the New World entitled *Les Singularitez de la France antarctique*; Pedro de Medina's Spanish-language classic *Regimiento de Navigacion*; and certainly less useful, Sir John Mandeville's colourful report of his imaginary travels in Asia in the fourteenth century. Several maps were purchased: most importantly, Mercator's 1569 map of the world illustrating the bizarre configuration of circumpolar islands, indrawing seas, whirlpool, and polar mountain and Abraham Ortelius's 1570 map showing a broad

Northwest Passage. The sum of £5, almost four times the price of the Mercator world map, was paid for a mysterious "very great carte of navigation." This may have been the chart drawn by William Borough of the Muscovy Company, with the apparent help of John Dee, which delineated the supposed islands of the north-western Atlantic and was used to plot the courses and discoveries of the voyage.

The list of navigational instruments purchased for the expedition included

— a greate globe of metal in blanke in a case of Leather
— a great instrument of brasse named Armilla Tolomei or Hemisperium
— a great instrument of brasse named Sphera Nautica with a Case
— a great instrument of brasse named Compassum Meridianum, with a case
— a great instrument of brasse named Holometrum Geometricum with a Case
— a great instrument of brasse named Horologium Universale, with a case
— a ring of brasse named Annulus Astronomicus
— a little standing level of brasse
— a case with small instruments for geometrie, of yron
— an instrument of wood, a stafe named Balistella, with a case
— a Astrolabium
— 20 compasses of divers sorts
— 18 hower glasses

Some of these items were ordered from Humphrey Cole, the first engraver and instrument maker to establish himself in England and a craftsman whose brass instruments were as beautiful as they were complex. The exact nature and purpose of some of these objects is not clear, and it seems likely that the more sophisticated would have been beyond the competence of Frobisher and his officers. The instruments that would have been used most frequently were the hourglasses, to measure the time on each course in order to make dead-reckoning estimates of position; the compasses, to point direction, and the "Compassum Meridianum," which was probably an instrument to measure the deviation of the compass needle from true north; and the "instrument of wood, a stafe named Balistella," which was a simple cross-staff for measuring the altitude of the sun or the North Star in order to determine latitude. Introduced in England by John Dee, the cross-staff was easier to use and more accurate than the more complicated quadrants and astrolabes employed by earlier explorers. Another instrument not mentioned in this list but recorded in the logs and journals was the sounding lead, a heavy lead weight with a hollow filled with soft tallow in the base and a very long cord on the other end. When dropped from the rail of a ship, the sounding lead measured the depth of the water, and the mud or sand or shell that stuck in the tallow identified the type of seabed beneath the ship. This information would be especially useful on the homeward leg of the journey, for most mariners could identify their location on the continental shelves of Europe from the combination of depth and bottom indicated by the sounding lead.

Masters had been found for the two ships, Owen Griffyne for the *Michael* and Christopher Hall for the *Gabriel*. The hired crews consisted of two gunners, a trumpeter (for signalling, we may suppose), a boatswain, a cook, a cooper, a carpenter, a smith, a surgeon (the tailor absconded with his pay before the expedition set sail), and assorted mariners for a total of thirty-four men. Food, beer, brandy, firewood, coal, medical supplies, and other necessities were loaded aboard, and the expedition was ready to set out by early June 1576.

Before the ships leave the Thames, it is appropriate to note that the dates recorded in the logs and journals are based on the Julian calendar, which was ten days behind the calendar used today. The more accurate Gregorian calendar was instituted by Pope Gregory XIII only in 1582, and it was not adopted in England until the eighteenth century. Here we follow the dates used in Frobisher's time, but in comparing seasonal weather and ice conditions with those known today, we should remember to add ten days to the reported dates. June 7, the day of Frobisher's departure from London, would be June 17 in today's calendar.

The expedition's departure was interrupted twice before it gained the open sea. On the first day the pinnace collided with a ship anchored at Deptford in the Thames and required repairs to its bowsprit. The next day the vessels sailed downstream to Greenwich, where the Queen was in residence, and Christopher Hall

Portrait of Queen Elizabeth I
by John Bettes the younger
(National Maritime Museum,
Greenwich)

records, "The 8. Day being Friday, about 12 of the clocke we wayed at Detford, and set saile all three of us, and bare downe by the Court, where we shotte off our ordinance and made the best shew we could: Her Majestie beholding the same, commended it, and bade us farewell, with shaking her hand at us out of the window. Afterward shee sent a Gentleman aboord of us, who declared that Her Majestie had a good liking of our doings, and thanked us for it, and also willed our Captaine to come the next day to the Court to take his leave of her." The three tiny ships anchored off Greenwich, flying their pennants and firing their small cannons to attract the royal attention, to be eventually rewarded by a cordial wave from the window of the palace, is an image that is indelibly associated with the Frobisher venture. Many later explorers dropped down the Thames to travel farther and make larger discoveries, but none could report such a gracious leave-taking. There is no record of Frobisher's interview with the Queen, but the fleet anchored overnight off Greenwich and was four more days in the Thames before setting out into the North Sea.

We are fortunate that Christopher Hall, master of the *Gabriel*, kept a log of the voyage across the North Atlantic, noting for each watch of the day the wind, weather, distance travelled, and notable occurrences. The document has survived, and although it is a mariner's working record rather than a descriptive narrative, it gives us a rare first-hand insight into the daily activities and major events of the voyage. After leaving the Thames, the ships sailed northward up the eastern coasts of England, and by June 26 they had reached Shetland, where they went ashore to take on fresh water and to repair a leak in the *Michael*. From here Frobisher and Hall sent a letter to John Dee, expressing their appreciation for his attempts to teach them the navigator's art and regretting that they had not been better pupils. They were now north of 60° latitude, and the midsummer nights would have been bright enough to sail safely even in coastal waters. Accordingly, they set out that night into the northwest and made good progress with the help of several days of strong southeasterly winds. The *Gabriel* covered at least four or five leagues in most four-hour watches and in a few travelled up to nine leagues (twenty-seven miles or forty-three kilometres) for a very respectable average speed of about seven knots, or ten kilometres an hour.

The afternoon of July 4 was calm, and the pinnace, which may have been towed by the *Gabriel*, was sent off to catch fish. According to the sailing directions for reaching Norse Greenland from Norway given in the thirteenth-century Hauksbók, one sailed "north of Shetland so that one sights land only in clear weather, then south of the Faeroes so that the sea looks halfway up the mountainsides, then south of Iceland so that one gets sights of birds and whales from there." Frobisher's ships seem to have joined this route somewhere to the west of Shetland and south of the Faeroe Islands, and at this point, seven days' sail west of Shetland, the fleet must have been crossing the banks that extend southwards from Iceland.

There is no mention of soundings in the log, perhaps because the *Gabriel's* sounding lead had been lost when the line broke just west of Shetland, but the presence of seabirds and whales, along with changes in the colour and motion of the sea, would have told the mariners that they were in shallow waters where they could handline for cod or halibut.

Fresh fish was an important commodity for Elizabethan seamen. The provisions loaded in London comprised the following items: 7,642 pounds (3,500 kilograms) sea biscuit, 40 bushels (1450 kilograms) peas, 12 bushels (430 kilograms) oatmeal, 26 bushels (940 kilograms) wheatmeal, 1,300 pounds (600 kilograms) rice, 5½ bushels (200 kilograms) mustardseed, 11 oxen, net weight 5,292 pounds (2,400 kilograms), 600 stockfish (salt cod; about 2,400 kilograms), 5 barrels (500 kilograms) butter, 1 barrel (100 kilograms) cheese, 27 flyches (sides) bacon (about 500 kilograms), 2 hogshead (560 litres) vinegar, 2 hogsheads (560 litres) sweet oil, 3 hogsheads (850 litres) aqua vitae (brandy), 13 tuns (15,000 litres) beer, and 5 tuns (5,600 litres) wine. These provisions were to last the expedition a full year, probably on the advice of Muscovy Company mariners, who knew the dangers of being frozen in and forced to overwinter in northern regions. If this was the case, then for thirty-five men we can estimate that each would be provided every day with only about a quarter of a kilogram of ship's biscuit and about an equal amount of other cereal, half a kilogram of salt beef on meat days or salt cod on fish days, supplemented with cheese, butter, bacon, and peas, and one litre of beer, together with occasional wine and tots of brandy. The beer was probably expected to spoil after the first few months, so the ration would have been closer to four litres per man per day, which was the standard allowance of the time. If forced to overwinter, the crew would have been reduced to drinking water to quench their thirst. We may hope that other provisions were also provided at a rate which assumed that the voyage would last less than a year, since the amounts given above are very meagre compared with the standard Elizabethan naval ration of one pound (half a kilogram) of biscuit, two pounds (one kilogram) of salt beef, and one gallon (four litres) of beer per day. In any case, the chance to supplement such a diet with freshly caught codfish would not have been ignored, and we should not be surprised that the tiny pinnace set off to fish in the mid-ocean calm. Unfortunately, the decision was to have a terrible consequence for its crew.

The following four days saw a mix of calm, storm, rain, and fog with relatively slow progress through the low-pressure conditions that habitually hover over the southwestern coast of Iceland during the summer months. The pinnace may not have been taken in tow or may have set out again to fish in the calm conditions of July 8. On the evening of that day, however, the sailors aboard the *Gabriel* lost sight of her in the fog, and a strong wind came up overnight. By the following morning the sea was "mightily growne," and the tiny ship with its crew of four had disappeared, presumably swamped or capsized and lost.

Three days later Hall reports that "we had sight of the land of Friseland bering from us West northwest 16. leagues, and rising like pinnacles of steeples, and all covered with snow." He measured the latitude as 61°, which would place the ships on the mountainous eastern coast of Greenland. This is the same latitude as Bergen in Norway and the location of the glacier Hvitserk (White Shirt), mentioned as the Greenlandic landfall in Ivar Bardarson's directions for sailing due west from Bergen to the Norse settlements. Michael Lok, whose report was based on the accounts of men who returned from the voyage, recorded that on July 11 "they had sight of land unknowne to them, for they could not come to set fote theron for the marveilous haboundance of monstrous great ilands of ise which lay dryving all alongst the coast therof … And bearing in nerer to discover the same, they found yt marveilous high, and full of high ragged roks all along by the coast, and some of the ilands of ise were nere yt of such heigth as the clowds hanged about the tops of them, and the byrds that flew about them were owt of sight."

The southeastern coast of Greenland is a narrow fringe of precipitous mountains, holding back the massive dome of the Inland Ice, which covers the interior of the near-continent. The rugged and barren coastline is protected by a stream of floating ice carried southwards by the swift East Greenland Current: massive icebergs calved from glaciers in valleys where the Inland Ice breaks through the mountain barrier, floes of shore ice formed along the coast in winter and broken away during the summer melt, and thick pans of multi-year ice torn free of the circling polar pack off Greenland's northern shores. The English sailors, even those who had sailed the Muscovy Company route to Archangel and seen ships frozen in for the winter, cannot have had experience with such phenomena. The hulls of their ships were more fragile than those of later Arctic explorers, and sailing among ice is hazardous even for experienced mariners. Sea ice is as dangerous as rock, and sailing in ice is akin to navigating in a field of reefs ranging from thickly scattered boulders to archipelagos of islands, all of which are moving to wind and current in different directions from the ship. Frobisher's crew soon learned that the dangers of ice sailing are often compounded by fog. With poor visibility, the grinding and crashing of fast-moving ice, the scream of seabirds, and the sudden appearance of icebergs rising into the clouds, the sailors understandably longed for the comforts of the open sea.

On the *Michael*, which appears to have become separated from the *Gabriel* during the same storm that overwhelmed the pinnace, the will to explore died when the sailors found the Greenland coast. According to Michael Lok, they were "so compassed with monstrous high ilands of ice fleting by the sea shore, that they durst not approche with their ship, nor land theron with their bote. And so in great discomfort cast about with the ship the next day: and set their course bak agayn homward to London, where they arived the first day of September." Aboard the *Gabriel*, which was now sailing alone, Hall reported that on July 12 "Wee had much adoe to get cleare of the yce by reason of the fogge." Frobisher and Hall had identified the ice-protected coast as that of "Frisland," a large mid-Atlantic island which stretched from 61° to 65° latitude on the bogus Zeno chart, and which from there had found its way onto the Mercator world map that had been purchased for the expedition. These maps had displaced Greenland far to the north of its correct position, accounting for the misidentification on Frobisher's part. Whatever the name of the country the mariners had encountered, they were simply thankful to have escaped its grasp and found their way to open water. The joy was short-lived, for two days later, on July 14, they were struck by a northerly storm that almost put an end to the voyage, knocking the *Gabriel* on her side, flooding the hatches, and ripping apart the rigging. Only Frobisher's quick and courageous action saved his ship, and with only a tiny foresail set they "spooned afore the sea Southwest 15 leagues, till it was Sunday."

That day brought calmer winds, a ship that had been pumped dry, and rigging repaired to workable order. The decision was made to continue westwards whatever the consequence, and for two weeks the lone ship wandered about the Labrador Sea in variable winds and occasional ice. The crew sighted the west coast of Greenland in the early morning of July 22 and immediately steered away westward to avoid the stream of sea ice that is carried along that coast by the northward-flowing West Greenland Current. For six days they worked their way westwards in light winds and fog before sighting a land which Christopher Hall took to be Labrador and which lay behind "a great store of yce." Michael Lok's account states that "on the xxixth day of July the capitayn himself first had sight of a new land of marveilous great heith. The headland wherof he named Elizabeth Foreland in memory of the Quene's Majestie." After an unsuccessful attempt to approach the shore, they sailed northwards. On July 31 the weather cleared, and they sighted a headland to

Frobisher's landfall off eastern
Baffin island (photo Nick Newbery)

Icebergs such as this one in Frobisher Bay were a novel and impressive sight to sixteenth-century European mariners (photo Walter Kenyon).

the north which they named the North Foreland, but for ten more days they were prevented by ice, fog, and tidal currents from getting ashore or making headway to the west. During one calm afternoon, Hall hoisted out the ship's boat and rowed to a large iceberg in order to take soundings. The next day he learned the foolhardiness of such an undertaking when, safely back aboard ship, he watched the iceberg break apart, "making a noyce as if a great cliffe had fallen into the Sea."

Finally, on August 10, Hall reports that he was able to row ashore with four sailors in the ship's boat. They reached a small island and climbed to the summit before hastily returning to the distant ship by rowing against the current of a rapidly changing tide. George Best, whose account is based on later interviews with the participants, gives more weight to this small adventure. He reports that Frobisher instructed this first landing party to bring him anything it found "in token of Christian possession" of the land. This taking of tokens was performed as a first formal attempt to establish English ownership and use of the newly discovered country. However, a black stone that was picked up from the beach of what is still known as Little Hall Island was to have major consequences for the Frobisher venture.

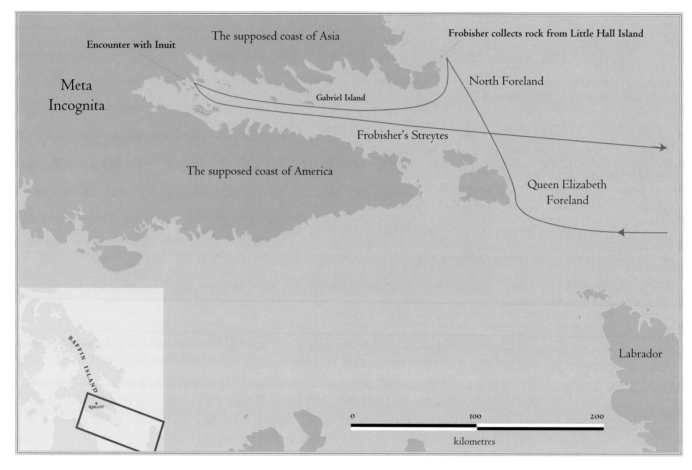

Meta
Incognita

Encounter with Inuit

The supposed coast of Asia

Frobisher collects rock from Little Hall Island

North Foreland

Gabriel Island

Frobisher's Streytes

The supposed coast of America

Queen Elizabeth
Foreland

BAFFIN ISLAND

IQALUIT

Labrador

0   100   200

kilometres

The next day the ice cleared sufficiently for them to enter the strait that stretched westwards between the two headlands they had discovered; on current maps these are marked as Resolution Island to the south and Loks Land to the north. Between these islands lies the entrance to what is now Frobisher Bay, a body of water about three hundred kilometres long and up to fifty kilometres wide, swept by the currents of a ten-metre tide and choked with ice for at least nine months of the year. The northern shore of the bay is a complex of islands and channels, backed by barren brown-green hills rising to about five hundred metres above sea level. The south-

Southern Baffin Island, showing the approximate route of Frobisher's 1576 voyage

ern shore is more strikingly severe, a straight bluff coast broken by short fjords, rising abruptly to grey peaks capped by the glistening domes of glaciers.

Frobisher was convinced that he had found a passage to Asia. According to George Best's account of the voyage, "that land uppon hys right hande, as hée sayled Westward, he judged to bée the continente of Asia, and there to bée devided from the firme of America, which lyeth uppon the lefte hande overagainst the same. This place he named after his name Frobishers Streytes, lyke as Magellanus at the Southweast end of the worlde, havyng discouvered the passage to the South Sea (where America is devided from the continente of that lande, whiche lyeth under the South Pole) and called the same straites Magellanes streightes." Over the next few days the explorers probed to the west, taking a day at anchor to caulk the *Gabriel* and naming the first large island they encountered after the ship. To the west of Gabriel Island they found that the open water narrowed and islands gradually encroached on the channel. By the time that they had progressed 60 leagues (280 kilometres) to the west of the first landfall, they found that "Frobishers Streytes" was almost blocked by a maze of islands separated by narrow channels swirling with tidal currents. Frobisher must have begun to fear that his passage was a dead-end bay or at least that he was entering an area of hazardous navigation. He and Captain Hall went ashore and climbed to the top of an island, hoping to identify a clear passage to the west. Michael Lok reported what they observed:

And on this western shore the capitayn with … his men went on shore on an iland mynding to have gone to the top of an high mountayn to discover what he could of the straiets of the sea and land about, and there he saw far the two hed lands at the furdest end of the straiets and no likelyhood of land to the northewards of them and the great open betwene them which by reason of the great tydes of flood which they found coming owt of the same, and for many other good reasons they judged to be the West Sea, whereby to pas to Cathay and to the East India.

How could mariners with the experience of Hall and Frobisher have convinced themselves that they had found a Northwest Passage in the narrow and island-studded inlet they had penetrated? Although both the Ortelius and the Mercator maps with which they were familiar showed a supposed channel to the north of the American continents, they pictured the channel as spanning over 100° of longitude and being several hundred kilometres in length. On the other hand, the measurement of longitude was largely guesswork to Elizabethan sailors, and in any case Frobisher knew that the length of the mapmakers' strait was purely hypothetical. Perhaps the most convincing feature of the body of water they were exploring was its resemblance to the strait that Ferdinand Magellan had discovered fifty years earlier at the southern tip of the Americas, a tortuous and dangerous channel three hundred kilometres in length separating the mainland from Tierra del Fuego. In an age in which arguments from divine symmetry were given authority, it must have seemed possible or even likely that a channel similar to the Strait of Magellan should lead from the Atlantic to the Pacific off the northern coast of America.

The navigators on their hilltop had little time for geographical speculation, however, for looking in the other direction they saw a small fleet of strangers approaching. The English were about to encounter the Inuit of Baffin Island, and the relations between the two groups would soon take an unfortunate turn that prevented any further exploration of Frobisher's Straits.

Five

THE FIVE LOST SAILORS

And being ashore, upon the toppe of a hill, he perceived a number of small things fléeting in the Sea a farre off, whyche hée supposed to be Porposes, or Ceales, or some kinde of strange fishe: but comming nearer, he discovered them to be men, in small boates made of leather.

George Best's account of the 1576 voyage

CHRISTOPHER HALL REPORTS THAT IT WAS A calm August morning when he and Martin Frobisher climbed to the summit of the small island. We may imagine it as one of those rare days in an Arctic August when the wind stops blowing and the still air is warmed by the sun, the mosquitoes have disappeared after an early frost, and a great clear calm hangs over the immense landscape. The ankle-high tundra vegetation stretching down the hillside would have taken on its autumn colouring from the brilliant yellow leaves of dwarf birch and willow, the red of blueberry bushes, and the brown of heather, the entire countryside resembling an enormous and intricate Persian carpet. To north and south the coasts of what Frobisher took to be Asia and America rolled away in barren rocky hills to distant horizons. Open water stretched into the northwest, flanked by two high ridges, and if the day was not perfectly clear, they would not have seen the low-lying country that enclosed the end of the bay 30 kilometres away. The tidal currents seething through the narrow straits between the islands produced great lines of choppy water and sinister, calm whirlpools, the huge tide suggesting in Frobisher's mind a through passage to the west. Unfortunately, the "infallible rules" that Humphrey Gilbert had claimed for distinguishing a closed bay from an open strait did not help Frobisher in this situation.

The first encounter with the Inuit occurred among the islands near the western end of Frobisher Bay (Canadian Museum of Civilization; photo Robert McGhee).

He and Hall had more immediate concerns – the men in small boats whom they had spotted from the hilltop. Seven kayakers were paddling towards them from the east, having probably seen the ship when it passed, and were now approaching to make contact with the newcomers. The Englishmen tumbled down the hill to reach their boat before the strangers arrived and rowed quickly back to the safety of their ship. The written accounts differ on what happened next, but we will follow primarily Hall's first-hand report, which seems the most reliable. Frobisher and his men were on board the *Gabriel* making ready for defence, when the Inuit went ashore at a camp that the English had not seen. Hall then took the ship's boat to the shore, with a white flag indicating peaceful intentions, and gave each of the men a "thredden point" ("points" are the small metal terminal pieces attached to the ends of laces to prevent them from unravelling, an important element of Elizabethan clothing and, as it turned out, a desirable trade item with the Inuit). He then invited one Inuk aboard the ship and left one Englishman ashore as hostage, the same arrange-

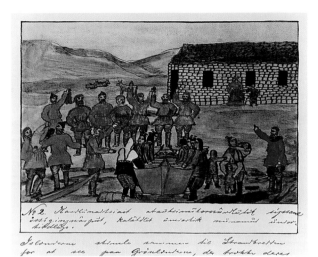

No 2. Kavdlunatsiait abastsimutkorsiutlictsit tigesaue essiginmuargut, Kaleldlit saeiorlik minamud sauor dilelilgo.

Islomune ahindu saumne til Straudbretten for at ree paa Gronlandeine, da trobbe deres

This painting by the nineteenth-century Greenlandic artist Aron of Kangeq illustrates Inuit historical accounts of meetings with the Norse (from *Kavdlunatsianik: Nordboerne og Skraelingerne* [Eigil Knuth 1968]; photo Harry Foster)

ment by which the young Martin Frobisher had been marooned in West Africa twenty-two years before. The Inuk who had come aboard the *Gabriel* was given food and wine, neither of which he enjoyed, but when he was taken back ashore, he was able to assure his countrymen that the strangers meant no harm. Soon nineteen Inuit had arrived aboard the ship, women as well as men and inevitably children also. They appeared familiar with ships such as this. Far from fearing the foreigners who had arrived in a strange vessel from the empty sea, they were eager to trade and even competed with the mariners in acrobatics on the ropes of the ship's rigging. They probably knew the newcomers to be *qadlunaat*, a term that had originally been applied to the Greenlandic Norse, whom the Inuit had encountered sporadically for the past three hundred years. More recently, the term would have been extended to the Europeans who seem to have occasionally penetrated the area in search of trade or plunder.

The English, on the other hand, had never come across such people. Some of the crew might have voyaged to Muscovy, where they would have encountered the wild Norwegians and the Sami (Lapps) who occupied the coasts of the Barents Sea. Aside from that experience, their expectations about the humans whom they were likely to meet in distant countries and strange environments must have been bizarre by modern standards. Sir John Mandeville, whose book of eastern travels was the closest thing to ethnography in the *Gabriel*'s library, described such wonders as a country of one-legged men whose huge single foot served as a shade against the hot sun of that land, green people and yellow people, a country where the women grew beards and the men did not, and a race of knee-high humans who married at the age of six months and died at six years. He also told of cannibals who bought and fattened children as food, another region where men drank blood, and the land of Amazonia inhabited by fierce women warriors. Such tales implied that there was usually considerable danger to be expected from encounters with strange races. Given this sort of background, the Englishmen's distrust and fear of the Inuit is

Artist's reconstruction of the first meeting between Frobisher's crew and the Inuit of Baffin Island
(painting by Francis Back; photo Harry Foster)

easy to understand. Although their new acquaintances appeared to be fully human, the mariners marvelled at their appearance. Christopher Hall described the Inuit as follows, noting especially the tattooed faces of the women: "They bee like to Tartars, with long blacke haire, broad faces, and flatte noses, and tawnie in colour, wearing Seale skinnes, and so doe the women, not differing in the fashion, but the women are marked in the face with blewe streekes downe the cheekes, and round about the eyes."

Over the next days the two groups cautiously traded, sometimes ashore and sometimes aboard the *Gabriel*. George Best noted that Frobisher "had sundry conferences with them, and they came aborde his ship, and brought him Salmon and raw fleshe and fishe, and greedily devoured the same before our mens faces ... They exchaunged coates of Ceale, and Beares skinnes, and suche like, with oure men, and received belles, loking glasses, and other toyes in recompence thereof againe." Since neither party knew anything of the other's language, communication on anything more complicated than simple hospitality and barter was fraught with incomprehension and misunderstanding. The English thought that they were told about open sea lying only two days' paddling by kayak to the northwest. They even thought that they had hired one of their new acquaintances to pilot them through the nearby islands and onwards to the end of the strait. From this situation arose the unfortunate incident of the five lost sailors, which was to poison relations between the two peoples.

On August 20, the Inuk whom they thought they had engaged as pilot was taken ashore in the ship's boat to get his kayak. The five sailors manning the boat were instructed to set him ashore in sight of the ship, but they rowed around a point of land to the Inuit village. Neither they nor the ship's boat was seen again by the English. Michael Lok gives the most complete account of the incident:

But these foolish men, being five of them in all in the bote, having set on land this stranger at the place appointed: the capitayn being in the ship saw them quietly put of their bote, and immediately contrary to his commandment and charge geven they rowed furder beyond that poynt of the land owt of his sight, and there landed iii of them, and the other twayn rested in the bote a little from the land so as he saw them agayn, to whom owt of the ship they made signes and noyse as well as they could to call them to the ship. And immediately these two men with the bote rowed into the land agayn to their fellowes owt of his sight, and after that hower he never saw them, nor could hear anything of them. And thus the capitayn having lost his bote and five of his best men, to his great discomfort he still remayned with the ship there at anker all that day and next night hoping to here of them agayn. But he could not here or know anything of them: and thereby he judged they were taken and kept by force

Without his only boat and unable to bring the *Gabriel* close to shore for fear of grounding, Frobisher was helpless. He anchored and sailed nearby for two days, firing a cannon and blowing trumpets to recall the men. Unsuccessful in this, he tried another tactic. Although the Inuit camp had been moved elsewhere by August 22, several men in kayaks came from shore to meet the ship. Among them was the first man to have boarded the *Gabriel* several days before, who now made signs of friendship and invited the English ashore. The man was lured close to the ship with the promise of a large bell, and when he approached, Frobisher himself leaned over the rail and plucked the man and his kayak from the water. The Inuk was held as a hostage for the return of the English sailors, but they could not learn from him any news of their shipmates, and the other Inuit made no move to effect an exchange.

With no ship's boat and a crew of only thirteen tired and sick men, and thirty centimetres of snow having fallen on deck the night after the sailors disappeared, Frobisher abandoned the missing men and set sail for England on August 25. The Inuit hostage and his kayak now took on a new role, as proof to Queen Elizabeth that Frobisher had reached a far and strange land. George Best described him as "this new pray (which was a sufficiente witnesse of the Captaines farre and tedious travell towards the unknowne partes of the worlde, as did well appeare by this strange Infidel, whose like was never seen, red nor harde of before, and whose language was neyther knowne nor understoode of anye)."

The English assumed that their sailors had been captured and probably murdered by the Inuit. Given their expectations of meeting fierce and probably cannibalistic peoples unrestrained by Christianity, this seemed a likely conclusion. But Inuit

Artist's reconstruction of Frobisher taking an Inuit man hostage by lifting him and his kayak from the sea to the deck of the *Gabriel* (painting by Francis Back; photo Harry Foster)

history, passed from generation to generation down the centuries, tells a much different story. When the explorer Charles Francis Hall visited Frobisher Bay in the 1860s, he found that the Frobisher expeditions were well remembered in the oral history of the Baffin Island Inuit. One of the stories told of five sailors who had been marooned by their ship, and it is tempting to believe that these may have been the five men lost by Frobisher in 1576. Inuit history, however, claimed that the men were not captured but were left behind, and that the Inuit did not kill them but cared for them through the following winter. The tradition included the name of an Inuit leader, Eloudjuarng, who protected the *qadlunaat* and ensured that they were cared for and that the hunters brought them

The archaeological remains of ancient Inuit winter villages such as this testify to centuries of Inuit occupation of the Eastern Arctic (Canadian Museum of Civilization; photo Robert McGhee).

food. It was also remembered that they preferred caribou and hare to seal meat. The following spring the *qadlunaat* built a boat, which the Inuit helped them to launch, but it was early in the season and there was too much ice. The men froze their hands and returned to the Inuit, who took care of them once more. Finally, when the sea was free of ice, Eloudjuarng composed a song wishing them happiness and a good passage, and they sailed away. But they were never heard from again and may have perished in the cold sea.

We shall likely never know what happened to the five lost sailors. Neither the English assumption that they were captured and murdered nor the Inuit story that they had been accidentally or purposely marooned seems entirely plausible. The Inuit would certainly have been tempted to steal the ship's boat, but would have had no other reason to take the men hostage and might have been restrained from such action by hopes of continued trade. The elements of the incident described by Lok — the men rowing the boat around a point of land after setting their passenger ashore; three men being put ashore while the others remained in the boat; the other two then rowing out of sight once more — contain no hint of violence and, indeed, suggest voluntary action on the part of the Englishmen.

Perhaps we should try to imagine the motives of the five sailors, young men who for ten weeks had endured the cramped quarters of a cold, wet, pitching ship. They had lived on bad food and worse beer, and had slept huddled together on the hard deck of a tiny forecastle. They had been subject to the discipline of a captain famous for his temper and impetuous actions. For the past few days they had come to be acquainted with the most extraordinary people they had ever met, smiling strangers who brought them fresh fish, swung about in the ship's rigging, dressed in warm furs, were eager to trade furs and ivory objects that could easily be sold for a profit at home in England, and introduced the sailors to their shy, tattooed, and charming wives and daughters. An invitation to come ashore and further their acquaintance, as well as to walk freely on the dry tundra and drink clean water from a stream, may have been too enticing to resist.

Once they were ashore and in the Inuit settlement, the insistence of their hosts, combined with fear of punishment on their return to the ship, may have kept the sailors ashore longer than they had planned. The Inuit must have discussed the ease with which they could now obtain a valuable wooden boat, weighing the advantages and disadvantages of making such a move. The fate of the sailors would have been entirely dependent on the nature of the camp leader. If the traditional Inuit stories are to be believed, the men may have been fortunate in encountering a leader who not only spared their lives but made sure that they survived in the community. However, he may not have possessed the power to have the boat returned to Frobisher's ship, and the subsequent kidnapping of an Inuit man would likely have brought an end to any talk of compromise. By August 25, when Frobisher decided to sail for England, the fate of the five lost sailors was sealed. Whatever really happened, the incident was the key event that determined relations between Inuit and English for the rest of the Frobisher venture.

Six

A Token of Possession

THE VOYAGE HOME, DRIVEN BY EARLY AUTUMN gales, took only five weeks. In late summer the nights are beginning to lengthen in southern Baffin Island, and Martin Frobisher chose a sailing date at the new moon, which would have provided some light until the ship was well clear of strange lands. Sailing out of Frobisher Bay and passing to the east of Queen Elizabeth Foreland (Resolution Island), the mariners set course for the southeast. In three days they sighted Greenland, still identified as Frisland and still protected by floating ice, and a few days later they were off the south coast of Iceland. Here they encountered a storm during which one sailor was washed into the sea but managed to cling to a rope until Frobisher once again put his strength to use and pulled the man back aboard. Two weeks later they sighted Orkney, on October 1 anchored at Yarmouth, and a week after that arrived in London.

Michael Lok describes the arrival: "and so came to London with their ship Gabriel the ixth day of October and there were joyfully received with the great admiration of the people, bringing with them their strange man and his bote, which was such a wonder onto the whole city and to the rest of the realm that heard of yt as seemed never to have happened the like great matter to any man's knowledge." Lok continues his commentary with great praise for Frobisher's accomplishment, "so greatly appertayning to the benefit of this whole realme of England," and of his determination to continue his efforts "ontill he have brought the same to such perfection as is desyred." We may wonder how widely the arrival of the *Gabriel* was actually noticed or acclaimed, and to what extent Lok the promoter was simply preparing the way for the continuation of a project that had not actually accomplished its goal of locating a northwestern passage to Asia.

According to the account by George Best, Frobisher returned to praise for "the great hope he brought of the passage to Cataya, which he doubted nothing at al to find and passe thorow, in those parts, as he reported." Called to testify before a commission discussing the possible extension of the project, Frobisher is reported by Lok to have "vowched to them absolutely with vehement wordes, speches and oathes, that he had fownd and discovered the straits, and open passage by Sea into the South Sea called Mar del sur which goeth to cathai." Yet we may ask whether Frobisher's confidence in his newly discovered Frobisher's Straits was universal. Christopher Hall, the most experienced navigator aboard the *Gabriel* and the officer whose log contained daily accounts of noteworthy events, recorded no evidence of the likelihood of the strait continuing to the westward. Although he accompanied Frobisher to the summit of the hill where the captain descried two distant headlands that he took to mark the outlet of the passage to the Pacific, Hall made no mention of the sighting. The expedition's chief navigator may not have been convinced that they had found the hoped-for passage to Asia, and despite Frobisher's oaths and vehement promises, there was little talk of a Northwest Passage after the autumn of 1576.

If any doubt of the existence of Frobisher's Straits arose, however, it did not prevent Lok from drafting a charter for a new enterprise to be called the Company of Cathay. Under the terms of this document, the venturers were to have a monopoly on exploiting the resources (and peoples) of all seas, islands, and countries lying to the north and west of England. Lok was to be appointed governor of the company, while Frobisher was to be named admiral, and each of them was to receive in perpetuity 1 per cent of all materials imported to England as a result of the enterprise. The charter was never issued, and the Company of Cathay remained an informal association of adventurers lacking royal licence. James McDermott has recently and convincingly argued that the refusal of a charter was the inevitable result of Queen Elizabeth deciding to become a major investor in the project and not wishing her investment of £1,000 to be subject to corporate decisions that she might not easily dominate.

By January 1577 the goals of the enterprise had begun to shift from exploration to the seemingly more immediate and sure profits of exploitation. The focus of this new interest was a black stone that Hall's landing party had picked up "in token of Christian possession" from their first Arctic landfall on August 10, 1576. In George Best's account, Frobisher had sent the men ashore for such tokens, and "Some of his companye broughte floures, some gréene grasse, and one brought a péece of a black stone, much lyke to a seacole in coloure, which by the waight séemed to be some kinde of mettal or Mynerall. This was a thing of no accompt, in the judgement of the Captain at the first sight. And yet for novelty it was kept, in respect of the place from whence it came." Best goes on to tell an appealing story of Frobisher giving pieces of the stone as souvenirs to venturers and friends in London, and how the wife of one of the investors happened to throw a piece in the fire and then quench it in vinegar, after which she noticed that it "glittered with a bright Marquesset of golde." The gold refiners to whom it was shown confirmed that this was high-grade gold ore and promised immense profit to whoever could obtain more.

This tale is as improbable as it is charming, and Michael Lok's version sounds more likely if no more easily understood in hindsight. According to Lok, Frobisher, on his return to London, had given him the stone as the first thing he had found in the new land. A few weeks later Lok gave a piece of the stone to the official assayer in the Tower of London, who analyzed it and reported it to be worthless. The same result was returned by two other reputable assayers. Then in January 1577 Lok provided yet another piece to a certain Giovanni Battista Agnello, a shadowy Venetian assayer who had lived in London for some time and had written a book on alchemy a few years earlier. Agnello made three assays of the ore and showed Lok gold powder that he had recovered from each of them. When challenged as to why other analysts could not find gold in the stone, Agnello simply replied, "Bisogna sapere adulare la natura" (One must know how to flatter nature). The answer seems to have satisfied Lok, whose judgment may have been influenced by his need of a lure to attract investors for a second voyage.

We now enter a rather murky episode, known mainly from an account that Lok presented to the Queen on April 22, 1577. The document was obviously written to clear him of allegations that he had been involved in activities against the interests

The black rock that Frobisher took to England as a token of possession probably resembled this Baffin Island cobble sparkling with mica (Canadian Museum of Civilization; photo Robert McGhee).

Engraving of assayer at work, from *De re metallica* by Georg Agricola, first published in 1556, which was the principal text on mining and metallurgy at the time of the Frobisher voyages (photo Harry Foster)

of the Queen in the Northwest Passage enterprise. According to Lok, the assayer Agnello made him promise to keep secret his findings regarding the ore, and throughout the latter half of January Agnello and Lok had considered various means of obtaining gold ore without involving Frobisher. A scheme to send a ship to secretly mine ore was discarded, since only Frobisher and Hall knew of its location. The two men then thought that if a second expedition in search of a Northwest Passage were to take place, the ore might perhaps be loaded and carried home disguised as simple ballast and later find its way to the refining furnaces as the property of the conspirators. Another scheme involved sending a ship along on Frobisher's next expedition, under the pretext of undertaking a fishing voyage, and then loading it with ore once Frobisher had continued through the straits to Cathay.

By late January Lok was becoming concerned at being found out in such underhanded activities, and he approached Sir Francis Walsingham, the secretary of state and a member of the Privy Council. Walsingham requested samples of the "ore," which he submitted to several assayers, one of whom reported finding only a small amount of silver. Walsingham sensibly concluded that "Battista dyd but play the alchemist." For the next two months Agnello and Lok badgered Walsingham for royal support, but without success. On March 20 the secretary of state finally ordered Lok to let Frobisher in on the secret. Although Lok did so, he does not report the captain's reaction to the new information.

Meanwhile, apparently on a separate tack, Agnello convinced the naval commander and wealthy court official Sir William Winter that he could invest in an enterprise which would be much more profitable than even Lok had been told. The supposed value of the ore had now risen from £30 a ton, the figure given to Lok, to £240 a ton, which would pay a return of 2,400 per cent on expenses. With this new estimate, the court and the merchant community seem to have been speedily persuaded to support the venture. The Queen invested £1,000 on her own behalf, and Walsingham and Sir William Winter £200 each. By March 30 a total investment of £3,900 had been raised.

In hindsight, it is difficult to understand how such meagre evidence could have supported the interest and investment needed to send a second expedition to Arctic North America. If a promise of gold had not emerged, it seems doubtful that Frobisher's insistence that he had found a passage to Asia would have been sufficient to win the venturers a second chance. Even the promise of a Northwest Passage and of gold at the extremely high return of £30 a ton apparently did not sway the court to support the venture. But as we have seen repeatedly in more recent gold "plays," once the promised return on investment reaches a sufficiently high level, human greed inevitably overwhelms common sense. And common sense in Elizabethan England was influenced by a geographical outlook that expected distant and newly discovered countries to be replete with precious metals and stones. Spain had proved that the more southerly regions of America produced vast quantities of silver and gold, and more recently it had opened gold mines in the Phillipines, islands in the sea to which Frobisher's passage supposedly led. Jacques Cartier had found what he believed to be gold and diamond deposits on the shores of the St Lawrence River. Sir John Mandeville told of an Asiatic country where hills of solid gold were guarded only by a race of giant but easily tricked ants. We should not regard the

Elizabethans with condescension for allowing themselves to be swindled with such tales of riches. Similar incidents continue to occur in our own lifetimes, and even scholars have been known to invest in gold-mining ventures based on stories that were no more credible than those brought to Elizabeth's court.

With royal support, the enterprise was soon organized. Most of the Queen's investment was in the form of the *Aid*, a 200-ton ship that was to have a crew of 65 mariners, miners, soldiers, and "gentlemen." Together with the barks *Gabriel* and *Michael*, which had been used the previous year, Frobisher's fleet for the 1577 venture was to have a complement of 120 men, of whom about 30 were miners and assayers specifically employed to dig and load gold ore. Also on board was Jonas Schutz, a German assayer and mining engineer who had established a considerable reputation in pioneering mining ventures in England and had assisted Agnello in his assaying of the ore.

The ships were provisioned much as in the previous voyage but with the notable addition of "Provision for the apparrelling of the men: wollinge clothe for jirkens, breche and hose, canvas and lynnenge clothe for dublets and sherts, hats, caps, shewes, etc." at a cost of £100. Having experienced one Baffin Island summer, Frobisher was apparently willing to go to some expense to outfit his crew with more adequate clothing than had been provided for those who had accompanied him in 1576. Another addition to the 1577 voyage was a gang of convicts (an assortment of burglars, highway robbers, and horse thieves) who were to be marooned on the coasts of Frisland and Frobisher's Straits, together with supplies to overwinter, explore the country, and establish English footholds on these shores.

Frobisher also petitioned the Queen for an appointment as high admiral of the northwestern seas that he had discovered and would discover, along with a perpetual right for him and his heirs to a revenue of 5 per cent of all imports from the countries discovered in that region. The appointment, like the charter for the Company of Cathay, was never made. It seems that Frobisher was no longer viewed as a freelance privateer and adventurer but as a mariner engaged in the service of the Queen, who had provided him with his flagship as well as a significant personal investment to explore the newly discovered land.

In return for the support of the court, Frobisher was subject to the regulation and supervision of his patrons, and a detailed document was drawn up specifying the actions that he should undertake. The primary task of the *Aid* and its large complement was to locate and excavate gold ore, while the *Gabriel* and the *Michael* searched for further deposits, and then explored westward for the passage to the South Sea. If the outlet of the passage was not found within 150 leagues (700 kilometres), however, they were to return. Only if it turned out that the miners could not find any ore were the smaller ships to proceed to Cathay while the *Aid* returned to England.

Having received its instructions, the fleet sailed from the Thames on May 25, puting in at the east-coast port of Harwich to load further supplies. Here Frobisher received a final letter of instructions from the Privy Council, reminding him that he was to take no more than 120 men on the expedition. He had apparently exceeded this limit, probably for motives of private gain, but the general (as Frobisher is now referred to) complied with the instructions, discharging several men, "whych with unwilling myndes departed." Among those whom he put ashore, however, were the convicts who were to be marooned on Arctic coasts, and who must have been exultant at their reprieve. The rest set off northwards once again, this time with expectations of immediate wealth.

Seven

ICE, HOSTAGES, AND GOLD

MARTIN FROBISHER LEFT ENGLAND ON HIS SECOND voyage to the northwest on May 31, 1577, and a week later the fleet anchored off the Orkney Islands. The local inhabitants fled, expecting to be plundered, but eventually Frobisher convinced them that they had nothing to fear, and the crew was able to trade clothing, old shoes, and rope for fresh eggs, fish, and birds. The behaviour of the Orcadians is revealing in view of the very similar reaction of the Baffin Island Inuit whom the English were to encounter this summer. The peoples of isolated North Atlantic coasts, from northern Scotland to Arctic Canada, probably shared a warranted fear of ships appearing off their settlements and men coming ashore. For over a century English ships had harassed the coasts of Iceland, plundering isolated farmsteads of anything of value and kidnapping people to be sold into slavery as far away as North Africa. Similar ships must have visited the Shetland and Faeroe Islands and even on occasion Greenland and Labrador. The greeting that Frobisher had received from the Baffin Island Inuit the previous summer suggests that their prior experience of Europeans had been relatively friendly, but that was to change in the coming weeks.

After obtaining its provisions, the fleet set off northwestwards with "a merrie winde." The ships were probably following the homeward track of the previous year's voyage, although we must guess at their course since we lack the same navigational information as Christopher Hall's log provided for 1576. This time the ships had a definite destination, the source of the alleged gold-bearing rock at the entrance to Frobisher's Straits, and all attempts were made to keep the actual location of this valuable site secret lest foreign spies should be aboard or they later read accounts of the voyage. The lack of precise information is compensated for by the full and detailed description of this voyage published by George Best, who was listed as Frobisher's "Lieutenant" and was a man with a wide knowledge of geography, broad interests, and a writing style that is unexpectedly elegant and engaging for someone who purported to be a mariner. The passages quoted in this and the following chapters are, unless otherwise noted, from Best's account of the voyage.

For twenty-six days the fleet sailed out of sight of land, encountering only driftwood, whales, and seabirds. In the company of the *Aid*, the crews of the tiny barks *Gabriel* and *Michael* must have felt considerably more secure than they had the previous year. The *Aid* is the only one of Frobisher's ships for which a pictorial record has been preserved, in the form of a small detail in a watercolour depicting the naval battle of Smerwick Harbour in 1580. The painting shows a three-masted ship with square sails on fore and mainmasts and a triangular lateen rig on the mizzen-mast, a high stern castle with two decks above the main deck, and below this a gun deck with four gun ports on each side. In 1577 she would have been adapted for carrying cargo rather than fighting and would have made a safe and efficient ship for transatlantic voyaging.

On July 4 the small fleet struck the coast of Greenland, just to the north of its southern tip at Cape Farewell, and once again found fog and drifting ice extending from the land. For four days the ships edged along the ice, rounding Cape Farewell and sailing northwards along the west coast. We can guess that they continued north until they reached the latitude of their destination; then finding the Greenland coast still trending northwards, they struck out due west from about the location of the present-day community of Paamiut.

After a stormy crossing of the northern Labrador Sea, the mariners sighted land and soon recognized the North Foreland marking the northern entrance to Frobisher's Straits. More importantly, they recognized Little Hall Island, where the previous year Hall's landing party had picked up the celebrated black stone. Two small pinnaces were unloaded from the deck of the *Aid*, and Frobisher himself accompanied the assayers through the ice in hopes of finding a deposit of black ore. We can imagine their disappointment when they "could not gette in all that Iland a peece

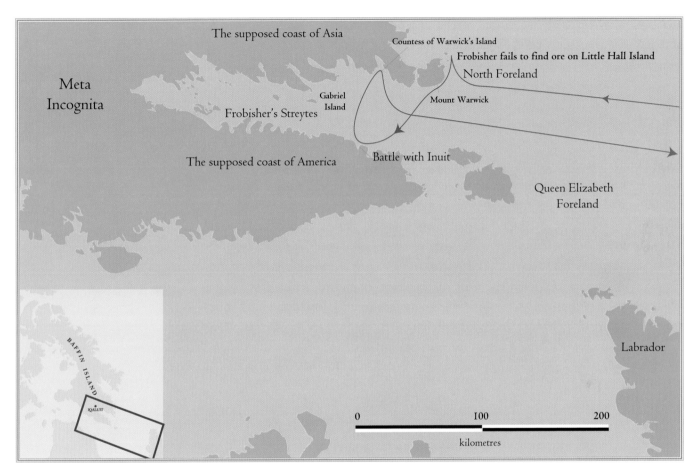

The supposed coast of Asia

Countess of Warwick's Island

Frobisher fails to find ore on Little Hall Island

North Foreland

Meta
Incognita

Gabriel
Island

Mount Warwick

Frobisher's Streytes

The supposed coast of America

Battle with Inuit

Queen Elizabeth
Foreland

BAFFIN ISLAND

IQALUIT

Labrador

0   100   200

kilometres

Southern Baffin Island, showing the approximate route of Frobisher's 1577 voyage

so bigge as a Walnut." However, the second boat visited nearby islands and found them all well supplied with ore, so the cannons were fired and there was general celebration when Frobisher returned in the late evening with fresh eggs, birds, and a seal that the party had killed ashore.

The general's first duty was to claim the newly discovered country and its potential riches for England. The procedure for claiming sovereignty over land not already possessed by another Christian ruler was well established in the Europe of Frobisher's day, a Europe still largely ruled by medieval concepts of authority and landownership by individual monarchs as deriving from God. By raising a cross and claiming the land in the name of God and their monarch, Europeans of the time considered that they had legitimized their assertion to ownership of the homelands of non-Christian peoples. Frobisher carried out this ritual on the summit of a prominent hill, which he named Mount Warwick, located at the northeastern entrance to Frobisher Bay:

on Friday the nineteenth of July in the morning earely, with his best companie of Gentlemen and souldioures, to the number of fortie persons, went on shoare … And leaving his boats here with sufficient guarde, passed up into the countrey about two Englishe miles, and recovered the toppe of a highe hill, on the top whereof our men made a Columne or Crosse of stones heaped uppe of a good heigth togither in good sorte, and solempnely sounded a Trumpet, and said certaine prayers, kneeling aboute the Ancient, and honoured the place by the name of Mount Warwicke … This done, we retired our companies, not seeing any thing here worth further discovrie, the countrie seeming barren and full of ragged mountaines, in most parts, covered with Snow.

This cairn stands on the summit of a high hill at the northern entrance to Frobisher Bay; it is relatively modern, but may have been built from the stones of Frobisher's cairn (photo Walter Kenyon).

The land claiming had not gone unnoticed by the Inuit, who appeared at the top of Mount Warwick waving a flag and calling out to the English as they descended the hill towards their boats. The two parties traded cautiously and invited each other to further hospitality, which was warily declined on both sides.

And thus marching towards our boats, we espied certaine of the countrie people on the top of Mount Warwicke with a flag, wafting us back againe & making great noise, with cries like the mowing of Bulles, seeming greatly desirous of conference with us: whereuppon the General, being therewith better acquainted, answered them again with the like cries, whereat, and with the noise of our trumpets, they seemed to rejoyce, skipping, laughing and dauncing for joy … So that forthwith two of our menne, and two of theirs mette togither a good space from companie, neither partie having their weapons about them. Our men gave them pinnes and pointes, and such trifles as they had. And they likewise bestowed on our men, two bowe cases, and suche things as they had. They earnestly desired our menne to goe uppe into their Countrie, and our men offered them like kindnesse aboorde oure shippes, but neyther parte (as it seemes) admitted or trusted the others curtesie.

The caution of the Inuit was well founded. Late on the same day that they had climbed Mount Warwick and traded with the natives, Frobisher decided to capture a man who could be used as an interpreter. Having made a successful seizure the previous year, he himself set out, accompanied by Christopher Hall, his companion of the previous summer and now master of the *Aid*. The two men feigned another trading arrangement like the previous one, but after making a few exchanges, they seized the two Inuit with whom they were dealing. Frobisher's grip was not as tight as on the Inuk he had lifted from the sea the previous summer, and the Inuit men escaped to the place where they had left their weapons and chased the Englishmen back to their boat. Frobisher received the first wound of the summer, being hit in the buttock by an iron-bladed Inuit arrow. He was revenged when the sailors from the ship's boat pursued the Inuit and captured one of the men, who was brought back to the ship as the first hostage of season. "And so beeing stayed, he was taken alive and brought away, but the other escaped. Thus with their straunge and newe praye oure men repaired to their boates, and passed from the maine to a small Ilande of a myle compasse, where they resolved to tarryie all night, for even now a sodaine storme was grown so great at sea, that by no meanes they coulde recover their ships."

The storm almost put an end to the expedition. The officers had apparently all gone ashore to take part in the ceremony of claiming possession, and were now marooned with few supplies on a tiny island. With the ships driven offshore and out of sight, the hungry men were considering their chances of reaching Newfoundland by boat if they were truly abandoned. On board the ships, the worried crews battled throughout the night to prevent the vessels from being sunk by collisions with the wind-driven ice. Their ultimate success they attributed to "God being our Steresman, and by the industry of Charles Jackman and Andrew Dyer then maisters mates, both very expert Mariners, and Richard Coxe the maister Gunner, with other very carefull saylors then within borde, and also by the helpe of the cleare nightes which are without darkenesse."

The storm abated the next morning, and the ships recovered their marooned officers, the mariners thanking God for their unexpected deliverance from such peril. They had seen enough of Davis Strait, however, and decided that whatever wealth could be obtained from the local islands would not be worth the risk of facing the winds and drifting ice of this exposed coastline. Accordingly, they turned the ships to the southwest, to try their luck on the southern shore of Frobisher's Straits. Here they discovered protected bays and plenty of rock, which they took to be gold and silver ore but found difficult to mine.

In one of the bays that they explored, the English found a stone tomb containing a skeleton. Assuming that "heathen savages" would not care for their dead in such a manner and that this must be the tomb of an Englishman, they demanded of their captive that he confirm that his countrymen had killed and eaten the person whose bones were buried with such care. The Inuk denied the charge and gave them to understand that the victim had been killed by wolves and other wild animals. Actually, he was telling them that this was a typical Inuit burial chamber and that the body placed here had been stripped of its flesh by animals. The English were diverted by finding a boulder-covered cache containing preserved fish as well as sleds, harnesses, kettles, knives, and the other accoutrements of an Inuit house-hold. The Inuk fitted a harness to one of the ship's dogs – this is the first mention of dogs being aboard; perhaps they had been stolen from an Inuit camp – and showed his captors how the animals were used to pull sleds. Having learned that dogs were used as draught animals, the English made the mistaken observation that the Inuit had two types of dogs, the larger used as horses and the smaller fattened for eating like domestic cattle in England.

The Inuit captive was also interrogated about the five sailors who had disappeared the previous summer. It is difficult to know how much of the communica-tion between the man and his captors was actually comprehensible and how much mistaken. The English thought they were told that their captive knew about the five sailors, that he vehemently denied that they had been killed and eaten, and that he reported that they were still alive and well. They came to the opposite conclusion a few days later when the crew of the *Aid* visited an abandoned Inuit camp, where they found a few items of European clothing: a canvas doublet, a shirt, a girdle, and three shoes of different sizes. Although this camp was more than two hundred kilome-tres from the place where the five sailors had disappeared the previous summer, the English assumed that the clothing belonged to their kidnapped countrymen. On the chance that the men might still be held captive by the people of this camp, they formed a battle plan.

A party of men was put ashore in an adjacent bay, from which they crossed the hills to surprise the people in the camp. When they arrived, they found that the tents had been taken down and the camp moved, but they discovered another small camp some distance up the bay. They decided to try to capture the people in this camp, but the sixteen or eighteen Inuit saw them coming from a distance and took to sea in a kayak and an umiak, a large skin-covered boat traditionally rowed by women and used for travelling or hunting whales. The soldiers fired their guns, attracting the rest of the English party, which was to attack from the sea, and the Inuit were forced ashore at a point of land the English aptly named Bloody Point. In the subsequent attack five or six Inuit were killed, and one Englishman seriously wounded. George Best gives a vivid description of the encounter:

The southern coast of Frobisher Bay, where the attack on the Inuit camp occurred, is a steep and heavily glaciated shore (photo Walter Kenyon).

And therupon indeede our men whiche were in the boates … forced them to put themselves ashoare upon a point of lande within the said sound (which upon the occasion of the slaughter there was since named the Bloudie point) whereunto our men so speedily followed, that they hadde little leysure lefte them to make any escape. But so soone as they landed, eche of them brake his Oare, thinking by that meanes to prevent us, in carying away their boates for want of Oares. And desperately retorning upon our men, resisted them manfullye in their landing, so long as theyr arrows and dartes lasted, & after gathering up those arrows which our men shot at them, yea, and plucking our arrowes out of their bodies, encountred afresh againe, and maintained their cause, until both weapons & life utterly failed them. And when they found they were mortally wounded, being ignorant what mercy meaneth, with deadly furie they cast themselves headlong from off the rocks into the sea, least perhaps their enimies shoulde receive glorie or praye of their dead carcasses, for they supposed us be like to be Canibales, or eaters of mans flesh.

Painting by the noted sixteenth-century artist John White, showing the skirmish between Inuit and Frobisher's men (British Museum)

Forcing their way ashore, the English found two women who had fled the attack and were hiding among the rocks. Suspecting that the older woman might be a witch, they removed her boots to check for cloven feet. Unconvinced, they left her behind, taking hostage a young woman carrying an infant son, who was shot in the arm during the capture.

Best's account of the skirmish is appalling not only for the matter-of-fact manner in which he describes the event but for what it reveals about English beliefs regarding the nature of non-European and non-Christian peoples. Assuming that the Inuit were totally unrestrained by society or religion, the English decided that they must be cannibals and could have no concept of mercy. Since during the summer the Inuit lived in tent camps, the English concluded that they were "a dispersed and wandring nation, as the Tartarians, & live in hords and troupes, withoute anye certayn abode … They live in Caves of the Earth, and hunte for their dinners or praye, even as the beare, or other wilde beastes do. They eate rawe fleshe and fishe, and refuse no meate, howsoever it be stinking. They are desperate in their fighte, sullen of nature, and ravenous in their manner of feeding." The English noted that the young mother whom they had captured cleaned the wound in her infant's arm by licking it as a dog would. They seem to have viewed the Inuit as we might observe a previously unknown species of strange, dangerous, and potentially entertaining animal. They were continually surprised by the human emotions and conduct exhibited by their prisoners and found it difficult to understand these as attributes shared by all peoples, rather than only by those whose character had been formed by European society and the Christian religion.

Observation of their hostages was an interesting diversion, but the English soon got down to their principal business. After looting the Inuit camp of "suche poore stuffe as they founde in their tentes," the men from the *Aid* returned to their ship and crossed to the north shore of Frobisher Bay. There the crews of the *Gabriel* and the *Michael* had found a small island containing a deposit of black rock, which they took to be gold ore. Just as importantly, the island provided a protected anchorage in ice-free waters, and its isolation granted some security from surprise attack. They named the island and the body of water surrounding it after Anne, Countess of

These prehistoric Inuit artifacts, excavated from archaeological sites in the eastern Arctic, are probably very similar to those found in the Inuit camps looted by Frobisher's crew; clockwise from upper left: two harpoon heads, one with polished stone blade; ivory thimble holder and needle case; fish lure; toggle in the form of two bear heads; bead; bird-woman figure; lamp trimmer; figurine; comb (Canadian Museum of Civilization; photo Merle Toole).

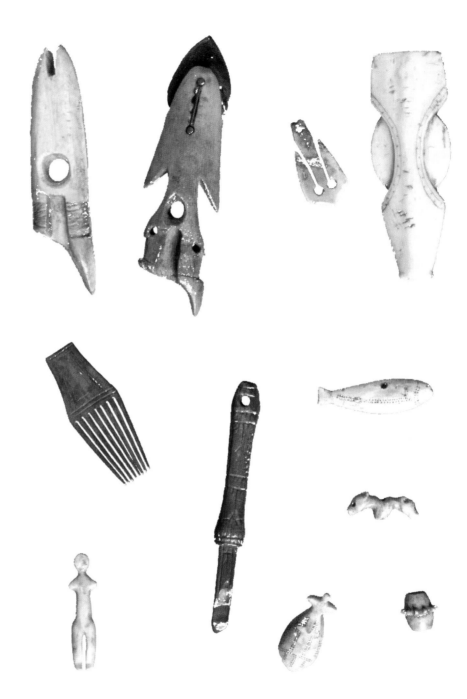

Warwick, who had invested £50 in the venture. On July 29 Frobisher himself set about mining ore. "And therefore our Generall setting the Myners to worke, and shewing fyrste a good president of a painefull labourer & a good Captaine in him-selfe, gave good examples for others to follow him: whereuppon every man, both better and worse, with their best endevors, willingly laide to their helping hands."

Two features of the Countess of Warwick's Island may have attracted the prospectors: a cluster of large black boulders still lies on its gravel surface and is noticeable from a considerable distance; as well, a wide vein of similar rock cuts through the sea cliffs on the island's northern shore. This vein could be mined from the beach by simply hewing at the face of the cliff, and the rock could be immediately loaded into boats without carrying it any distance. Jonas Schutz, the German metallurgist who had been hired as chief assayer of the expedition, seems to have considered the ore to be of mediocre grade. However, a decision was made to mine what could be taken from this relatively safe area, rather than to continue searching in the hope of finding richer ore.

The process of mining, as practised by Frobisher's crew, was less a skilled craft than brute labour with simple tools, probably only iron wedges, picks, crowbars, and sledgehammers. The goal would have been to break or pry from the cliff chunks of rock small enough to be hand carried or loaded into wicker baskets carried on the miners' backs. The rock would then be loaded into boats, rowed to the ship anchored a couple of hundred metres offshore, lifted in large baskets attached to a gantry, and tumbled into the hold, which had been previously emptied of ballast.

The mine produced by this labour forms a broad notch in the sea cliffs of the island to this day, and it is easy to imagine how it was worked. Less than a metre of gravelly soil covers the vein of rock. This would have been shovelled or pushed over the edge of the cliff, to be washed away by the sea, and then boulders would be hammered and pried from the bedrock until they fell to the beach below. To take advantage of the ten-metre range of local tides, the ore would have been loaded at close to high tide, when the boats could be brought almost to the base of the cliff. As the edge of the cliff receded under the miners' hammers, the floor of the open-pit operation was sloped upwards so that boulders could be rolled or carried downhill to the beach. Today the mine measures 5 metres wide and 4 metres deep at its lower end, and it slopes upwards over a length of 25 metres to the island surface. One side is formed by a vertical face of black rock, in which one can still trace the scars left by the miners' tools. Much of the work at this mine and at another on the surface of the island was probably carried out during the large expedition in 1578, but the mine at the cliff edge was almost certainly the first major excavation, begun in the previous year.

When the *Aid* returned from the southern shore of the bay with her captives and news of the skirmish with the Inuit, Frobisher began to worry about reprisal attacks. On August 6 George Best moved ashore with all forty soldiers in order to protect the miners. Three days later, after a party of Inuit had appeared on the adjacent mainland, they fortified a small peninsula on the island's eastern shore as a refuge in case of attack. "Best's Bulwark" was protected on three sides by steep sea cliffs, and the narrow neck of the peninsula was barricaded with casks full of earth.

The local Inuit were almost certainly unaware of what had occurred on the southern shore of Frobisher Bay a few days before, among neighbours whom they would not visit until winter ice provided a road for sled traffic across the bay. They soon discovered the English and began to visit the shores a few hundred metres from the Countess of Warwick's Island, but they seem to have been more interested in trade than in attacking the strangers. Frobisher assumed that they had come for the captured woman and child, so he placed her in full view at the summit of the island while he took the male captive ashore to negotiate an exchange of prisoners. The Inuk was overcome with emotion on meeting his countrymen, and we can assume that he told them about his captivity and the recent appearance of the other hostages. He then took the role of intermediary between Frobisher and the Inuit, although he cannot have learned much English in the weeks since his capture and his function as interpreter must have involved much guesswork on both sides.

As a result of this discussion, Frobisher thought that he had been told that the five sailors captured the previous year were still alive, and that the Inuit had offered to take a letter to them. The letter was duly written and sent off with the Inuit couriers the following morning, with a promise that they would return in three days.

George Best thought the contents of the letter worth recording:

The forme of Martin Frobishers letter to the Englishe Captiues

In the name of God, in whom we al beleve, who I trust hath preserved your bodyes and soules amongst these Infidels, I commend me unto you. I will be glad to seeke by all meanes you can devise, for your deliverance, eyther with force, or with any commodities within my Shippes, whiche I will not spare for your sakes, or any thing else I can doe for you. I have aboord, of theyrs, a Man, a Woman, and a Childe, which I am contented to deliver for you, but the man which I carried away from hence the last yeare, is dead in ENGLAND. Moreover, you may declare unto them, that if they deliver you not, I wyll not leave a manne alive in their Countrey. And thus, if one of you can come to speake with me, they shall have eyther the Man, Woman, or Childe in pawne for you. And thus unto God, whome I trust you do serve, in hast I leave you, and to him we will dayly pray for you. This Tuesdaye morning the seaventh of August. Anno. 1577.

Yours to the uttermost of my power

Martin Frobisher

I have sente you by these bearers, Penne, Incke, and Paper, to write backe unto me agayne, if personally you can not come to certifye me of your estate.

This mixture of pious thoughts and threats of genocide produced no results. When the Inuit returned, they brought neither the English captives nor a reply to Frobisher's letter. They continued to show an interest in trade, offering an inflated sealskin whaling float, which was exchanged for a hand mirror and was supposedly intended for the Inuit captives to use to store drinking water. However, the English suspected that it was really intended to be used as a swimming float to help the hostages escape, which they had almost accomplished on their own in one of the ship's boats. During several encounters over the following days, the English were wary of the apparently hostile intentions of the Inuit. In turn, they tried to wound the Inuit with their guns in order to impress them with the power of English weapons. Although there were no further deaths or kidnappings, mutual hostility between the two peoples prevented any further trading or exchange of information.

By late August the English had loaded two hundred tons of ore, and both the men and the equipment were badly worn from the labour. "And upon Wednesday at night, being the one and twentith of August, we fully finished the whole worke. And it was now good time to leave, for as the men were wel wearied, so their shoes and clothes were well worne, their baskets bottoms torne out, their tooles broken, and the shippes reasonably well filled. Some with over-straining themselves received hurtes not a little daungerous, some having their bellies broken, and other their legges made lame. And about this time the Ice began to congeal & freese about our ships sides a night, which gave us a good argument of the Sunnes declyning South-ward, and put us in minde to make more hast homeward." The following day the men dismantled their tents, built a bonfire at the summit of the island, marched behind their flag around the island, fired a farewell volley, and boarded their ships.

The fleet set sail for home on August 23, carrying its three hostages from the only world they had known. By the following evening the ships had cleared Queen Elizabeth Foreland and set their course more southerly than in the previous year in order to reach warmer latitudes. In a stormy passage the *Michael* lost company with the other ships, the master of the *Gabriel* was lost overboard, and the rudder of the *Aid* was so badly damaged that underwater repairs had to be made at sea. The *Aid* arrived off Lands End on September 17, but in stormy winds she could not make a safe harbour until six days later, when she finally entered Milford Haven in Wales. Sailing on to Bristol, her crew found the *Gabriel* already arrived at that port, having been guided in by a local ship since the loss of the master had left her with no competent navigator. They also heard that the *Michael* had arrived safely in Orkney, having followed the course of the previous year.

Frobisher rode to London to be received by Queen Elizabeth, who commended his accomplishments and gave the name Meta Incognita (Unknown Boundary) to the new land that had been claimed on her behalf: "And bicause that place & coun-try, hathe neuer heretofore bin discouered, and therefore had no speciall name, by which it might be called & known, hir Maiestie named it very properly Meta Incognita, as a mark and bounds utterly hitherto unknown." The precious ore was off-loaded from the *Aid* and stored under heavy locks in Bristol Castle. The Inuit hostages were taken ashore and introduced to a world that must have been beyond their comprehension. They were entering an exciting, terrifying, and startlingly brief period of their lives.

Eight

INUIT IN ENGLAND

IN 1566 THE CITIZENS OF THE GERMAN city of Augsburg encountered colourful posters entitled "True Portrait of a Savage Woman with her Little Daughter found in the District called Nova Terra and Brought to Antwerp and Recently Publicly Seen there and Still to be Seen." The carefully engraved illustration portrays a woman and child in distinctive Inuit clothing and with blue facial tattoos. They are described in the accompanying text as having been captured that year by the French in the recently discovered territory called Nova Terra, and it is stated that during the capture the woman's husband was killed, despite the fact that he was twelve feet tall and in the past twelve days had killed a dozen Frenchmen and Portuguese for food. By the time the poster was engraved, the woman and child had endured their stay in Europe for at least eight months and had learned some French. Rare copies of the handbill are the only surviving record of these first Inuit to have been brought to Europe during the age of exploration. The man whom Frobisher had kidnapped from his kayak in 1576 was therefore not the first Inuk to reach Europe. A portrait painted by the Flemish artist Lucas de Heere exists, but otherwise we know only that the captive barely survived the voyage to England, where he "died of colde which he had taken at Sea." We do not know the man's name, only that he was buried at St Olave's Church in London.

The three captives taken in 1577 survived only a few weeks longer, but more information about their character and experiences was recorded. The man's name is usually given in English as "Calichough." The woman's name, "Ignorth" or "Egnock," is probably a corruption of the Inuktitut word for woman, *arnaq*, while the name of the infant, "Nutiok," is certainly a corruption of *nutaraq*, the word for child. The man was

This imaginative engraving of Inuit life was used to illustrate an account of Frobisher's 1577 voyage; the original drawing may have been based on the Inuit hostages in Bristol (from Stefansson and McCaskill 1938; photo Harry Foster).

captured from a community that appears to have spent the summer on the outer islands at the northeastern entrance to Frobisher Bay. The community from which the woman and child were taken had summered on the southern shore of the bay, over a hundred kilometres away. The man and the woman had likely never met, although they must have spoken very similar dialects, may have had a few common acquaintances, and perhaps were able to trace a vague kinship through distant relatives.

When they were thrown together on the deck of an English ship, Inuit manners for greeting a stranger were tempered by their shared anxiety and incomprehension of the situation. For their part, the English eagerly anticipated the initial meeting of the two Inuit. "Having now got a woman captive for the comforte of our man, we brought them togither, and every man with silence desired to beholde the manner of their meeting and entertaynment, the whiche was more worth the beholding, than can be well expressed in writing." The English were obviously disappointed when no sexual interaction occurred. The couple simply stared at each another in mutual despair, before the woman broke the silence with a song and the man with a long and solemn speech, probably relating the history of his captivity.

Having become acquainted, the Inuit were provided a cabin and set to live as a family. George Best comments,

(I thinke) the one would hardly have lived, without the comfort of the other. And, for so muche as we could perceive, albeit they lived continually togither, yet did they never use as man and wife, though the woman spared not to do all the necessarie things that apperteyned to a good huswife indifferently for them both, as in making cleane their Cabin, and every other thing that apperteyned to his ease: for when hee was Seasicke, shee would make him cleane, she would kill and flea the Dogges for their eating, and dresse his meate ... and he likewise in al the meates whiche they did eate togither, would carve unto hir of the sweetest, fattest and best morsels they had.

The mutual care and affection of the captives astonished the English, who obviously expected something less than human behaviour from such wild and "uncivilized" people. "They are excéeding friendly and kinde harted one to the other, &

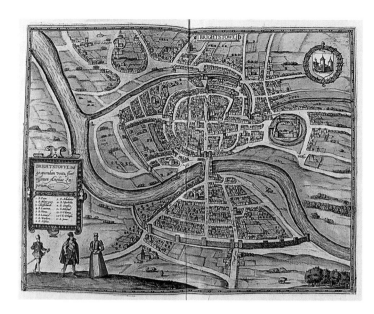

Engraving of the city of Bristol in 1580; "The Back," where the Inuit man hunted from his kayak, is near the bridge at the centre of the map (Bibliothèque de l'Assemblée nationale, Québec).

mourne greatly at the losse or harm of their fellowes, and expresse their griefe of minde, when they part one from an other, with a mournefull song, and Dirges."

The Inuit spent most of their time in England in and around the western seaport of Bristol, where the *Aid* and the *Gabriel* landed their cargoes of ore. Here the man hunted for food, using a kayak and a bird spear on the River Avon and providing one of the more memorable pictures of native North American prisoners in Europe. When he demonstrated his skill at a reception held by the mayor of Bristol, the occasion was sketched by an artist, and versions of the engraving made from the sketch were published in many European countries. The scene was also described in the annals kept by a local Bristol historian:

1577. Captaine Frobisher in a ship of our queenes of the burden of 200 tonnes came into Kingrode from Cattai, who brought certaine oare from thence, which was esteemed to be very ritch and full of gowld … They brought likewise a man called Callicho and a woman called Ignorth. They were savage people and fed only uppon raw flesh. The 9th. of October he rode in a little bote made of skinne in the water at the backe, where he killed 2 duckes with a dart, and when he had done carried his bote through the marsh upon his back. The like he did at the weare and other places, where many beheld him. He would hit a ducke a good distance of and not misse. They died here within a month.

Only a few scattered remarks hint at the lives these people had led aboard ship and later in England. The reference to their killing and eating "Dogges" while aboard the *Aid* suggests that they found English food inedible, a normal reaction to what is now known as culture shock. Inuit traditionally considered dog meat to be strictly emergency rations, to be eaten only as a last resort. Their English captors could not allow the Inuit to hunt for their own food lest they take the opportunity to escape, and the English were probably unable to capture seals or other animals for their prisoners' use. We know that they had stolen dogs from an abandoned Inuit camp, and it may have been these animals that were eaten on at least one occasion as preferable to the alien taste of salt beef and ship's biscuit.

Having arrived in England, the Inuit could no longer be considered prisoners capable of making an escape. Instead, they seem to have been placed in the role of valued guests, hosted and protected by the mariners with whom they had become acquainted during the voyage. Aside from their value as evidence that Frobisher had journeyed to a distant land, such strangers would have been the objects of great curiosity in Bristol society. On the basis of George Best's descriptions, it is apparent that mutual respect and even affection soon developed between the captives and their hosts.

These people are in nature verye subtil, and sharpe witted, readie to conceive our meaning by signes, and to make answere, well to be understoode againe … They will teache us the names of eache thing in their language, which we desire to learne, and are apt to learne any thing of us. They delight in Musicke above measure, and will kepe time and stroke to any tune which you shall sing, both with their voyce, heade, hande and feete, and wyll sing the same tune aptlye after you … They wondred muche at all our things, and were afraide of our horses, and other beastes, out of measure. They beganne to growe more civill, familiar, pleasaunt, and docible amongst us in a verye shorte time.

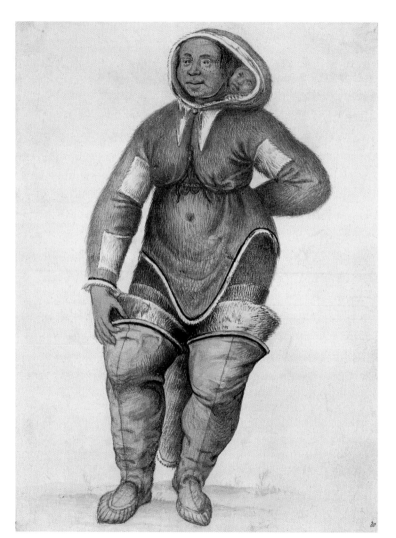
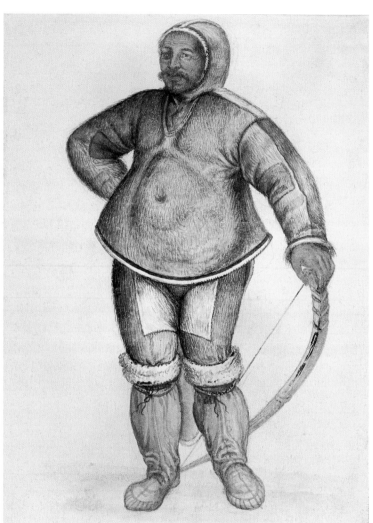

Portraits of the three Inuit captives by John White (British Museum)

Portraits of the Inuit painted by the artist John White are now in the British Museum. The man is shown in a conventionally confident pose, with hand on hip and a very European-looking bushy moustache. The woman's features are more Inuit-like, her face marked with blue tattoo lines, and her infant son peers over her shoulder from the hood of his mother's amautik. Other portraits seem to have been painted, but these have long since disappeared.

Most of the other information on these people relates to their deaths. When the man fell ill, a Dr Edward Dodding was called in and reported as follows: "At the first attack of the disease, when his strength was still intact, I was summoned, and with great force urged bloodletting, so that the stings of the inflammation would lie deadened and the matter would be lessened and overcome. But it was forbidden by the barbarous man's stupid, excessively barbarous timidity, and the advice of those with whom he was sailing prevailed with me." Obviously, both the Inuit man and his English hosts had a less barbarous view of human anatomy and medicine than the surgeon. When the man eventually died, the doctor blamed his death on the misguided kindness of his companions in providing him with too much food, as well as protection from medical care. In fact, an autopsy indicated that he had died of a lung infection associated with two ribs which had probably been broken when he was first captured and had not healed properly. He was buried without ceremony, supposedly so that the surviving woman would not think that he had been sacrificed by the English, and she was forced to watch the entire burial to assure her that the body was not being used as food.

The woman had a skin rash on the day of the burial and died a few days later of what may have been measles. The parish register of St Stephen's Church, Bristol, contains the following entry: "Burials in Anno 1577: Collichang, a heathen man buried the 8th of November. Egnock a heathen woman buried the 13th of November." The baby survived his mother and was taken to London in the care of a nurse, to be viewed by Queen Elizabeth. However, the child also fell ill, and despite medical attention, he died before he could be presented to the Queen. He was buried in the same London churchyard that contained the remains of the man who had been captured the previous year.

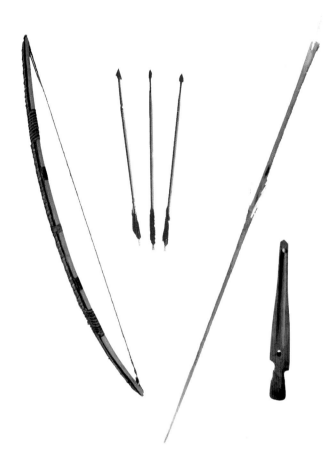

Early-twentieth-century Inuit bow, arrows, bird spear, and throwing board; the artists who portrayed sixteenth-century Inuit must have based their drawings on objects much like these (Canadian Museum of Civilization; photo Merle Toole).

These four unfortunates were probably the first Inuit to reach England, but they would be followed in later centuries by other people taken captive as souvenirs or persuaded to undertake the adventure of their lives by visiting the homelands of the whalers, traders, and missionaries who increasingly frequented Arctic shores. Most such visits ended in rapid death, since the Inuit lacked immunity to the European diseases they encountered in the unhealthy living conditions of English seaports. Only during the past half-century has extensive contact with Europeans ceased to pose a significant danger to Inuit health. In Frobisher's time, to be taken to Europe was an automatic sentence of death for the peoples of Arctic North America.

Nine

CREATING A GOLD PLAY

WHILE THE CAPTIVE INUIT WERE STRUGGLING to stay alive in England, the leading partners in the 1577 voyage began to take stock of their venture. The accomplishments of the expedition had been rather limited: the passage to Cathay had not been discovered; no Englishmen had been settled in the newly discovered lands, nor had the mariners established friendly and profitable relations with the natives of the country; and they had returned with a cargo consisting solely of three captives and two hundred tons of rock that had yet to be evaluated as gold ore.

Martin Frobisher himself rode cross-country from Milford Haven, where the *Aid* first made harbour, in order to report directly to Queen Elizabeth at Windsor. According to George Best, this hasty trip was undertaken "to advertise hir Maiesty of his prosperous proceeding, and good successe in this last voyage, and of the plenty of gold Ore, with other matters of importance which he hadde in these Septentrionell partes discovered." We must imagine that these facts were delivered with enthusiasm, if not with some degree of embellishment, in view of the enthusiastic response of the Queen and her Privy Council. Frobisher "was courteously enterteyned, and hartily welcomed of many noble men, but especially for his great adventure, commended of hir Maiestie, at whose hands he receyved great thankes, and most gratious countenance, according to his deserts."

The Queen and council must have been convinced of the value of Frobisher's cargo, for the black rock from Baffin Island, the country that the Queen named Meta Incognita, now began to be treated as if it was solid gold, and specific instructions were issued for its safekeeping. The larger quantity of ore, from the holds of the *Aid* and the *Gabriel*, was to remain in Bristol Castle under four locks, keys to which were to be held separately by Sir Richard Barkley, Frobisher, Michael Lok, and the mayor of Bristol. The cargo of the *Michael*, which had come to harbour in the Thames, was to be placed in the Tower of London, where it was to be protected with similar security. A royal commission was established, with the appointment of "special Commissioners, chosen for this purpose, Gentlemen of great judgement, art and skill, to looke thorowly into ye cause, for ye true trial & due examination therof, & for the full handling of al matters therunto appertaining."

Within two weeks of Frobisher's return, the commissioners were carrying out their responsibilities. Arrangements were made for the construction of a small smelting furnace on the property of Sir William Winter, who was one of the commissioners as well as an investor in the voyage and whose premises near Tower Hill were convenient for the purpose. Here Jonas Schutz, the head assayer of the 1577 voyage, was set to work making a proof of the ore in order to assess its value. The trial of a hundredweight of black rock was carried out on October 30, and Schutz reported that the ore contained 13 ounces of gold per ton, valued at £40 a ton. A second assay that he carried out a month later produced identical results. This amount of gold meant that the rock was high-grade ore, promising an excellent rate of return and therefore well worth the mining and smelting.

Sir Francis Walsingham, the secretary of state and the court officer to whom the venturers reported their findings, thought it prudent to have an independent assay made, and he assigned the project to Burchard Kranich. Like Schutz, Kranich had received his training in mining and metallurgy in his native Germany. For over twenty years he had lived in England, where he had opened silver mines unsuccessfully in Cornwall. In recent years, however, he had practised as a physician in London, where he was also known as Dr Burcott. Kranich tested a hundredweight of "black ore" and on November 26 reported to Walsingham that it contained 10 ounces of gold per ton, while a similar test on "red ore" (from a Baffin Island location known as Jonas' Mount, probably discovered or selected by Jonas Schutz) produced a measure of 40 ounces per ton. Both ores could be very profitably mined at this rate, and Kranich petitioned Walsingham to appoint on an annual salary "some expert and skilful man in the knowledge of minerals that if any such rough, wild and foreign ore at any time hereafter happen to come into this land, that he by his true assays thereof may certify her highness of the same at his own charges, that thereby her Majesty and subjects may not (as heretofore they have been) be deceived by such vain and untrue reports." His reference to untrue reports is unclear, but subsequent disagreements between Kranich and Schutz suggest that it may refer to the latter's assays of Frobisher's ore.

The two assayers were brought together in early December, but the attempted collaboration was not a success. Each man immediately began to criticize the techniques, knowledge, and competence of the other, creating a rivalry that may have contributed to the increasingly bizarre results of further assays which they carried out over the winter of 1577–78. Other assayers were also contracted to undertake small-scale tests. The first to be reported was made by Giovanni Battista Agnello, whose original tests on the stone brought back from Baffin Island in 1576 had initiated the quest for gold. The assay was carried out in January 1578, and "yt succeeded not well," producing no indications of any precious metal. A similar small test was made by another assayer, John Wolfe, with an identical outcome. A Huguenot apothecary named Geoffroy Le Brumen was provided with a small sample of ore and also found no gold.

In February, Schutz undertook another test using two hundredweight of ore. While working on this assay at the furnace that he had built on Winter's property, he became the target of Martin Frobisher's temper. Apparently infuriated by delays in the assay at a point when time was critical for the organization of a third expedition, Frobisher visited the assayer at his work on February 15, and according to Michael Lok's later account, "He drew his dagger and furiouslye ranne upon Jonas [Schutz], beinge in his worke at Tower hill, and threatned to kill him yf he did not finishe his worke owt of hand, that he might be sett owt againe on the thirde voiage, whereuppon Jonas did conseave so eavell nature in him, that he made a sollempe vowe he would never go to see any more with him, which hath byn no small domage to the Company in the ewre brought home the thirde voyage." This visit may have had a negative influence on Schutz's work, for the results that he produced three

weeks later were considerably poorer than any he had obtained in earlier assays —
only 2.6 ounces of gold per ton.

While Schutz was working at Sir William Winter's house, Burchard Kranich had
been contracted to make a further test on a hundredweight of ore at his own premises, and this assay proved the turning point for future plans. On February 21
Kranich announced that he had found 13.5 ounces of gold per ton, as well as a bonus
of over 50 ounces of silver, thus surpassing any of Schutz's results. The outcome
was questioned by Robert Denham, a metallurgist who had been assigned by the
commissioners to assist Kranich and who obviously also served as their spy. According to Denham, Kranich separated the metals by adding another material which he
referred to as "ore of antimony" and which he claimed contained no metal. However, Denham obtained and tested a sample of the "antimony" and found it to contain silver, copper, and lead, suggesting that the assayed silver came from this source
and not from Frobisher's ore. More alarmingly, Denham alleged that the assay had
been done on a single pound of ore, and that Kranich had then added his own gold
and silver to make up the proportions for the full hundredweight. Kranich admitted to the additions, but claimed that the proportions were based on a larger sample of smelted ore, which included all but a portion of the ore that had been ruined
through Denham's incompetence. We might expect that the problems surrounding
this assay would have caused unease among the venturers, and Michael Lok later
charged that Frobisher "did practyse to advance D. Burcot [Dr Burcott, i.e., Burchard Kranich] into the place of Jonas [Schutz], & mayntan Burcots false proffes
made of the ewre, to thend he might be sett on agayn in this third voyage, as the
Commissioneres and Denham canne witness." Whatever the motives of Frobisher
and the commissioners, it was largely on the basis of this questionable assay that a
third and larger expedition was organized in the spring of 1578.

Financial considerations were as important as the testing of ore in deciding
whether a further voyage could be undertaken. Throughout the autumn and winter
of 1577–78 the raising of funds was intimately linked to the hopes of the partners
and the promises of the assayers. Frobisher's first voyage of 1576 had overspent the
funds subscribed by its backers, and the shortfall had been made good by Lok from

his own pocket. This amount had to be repaid from the financing of the 1577 voyage, which also suffered from the nonpayment of several promised subscriptions, primarily by individuals at court. Once the deficit from 1576 had been repaid (largely through the expedient of selling the ships and their gear to the new expedition at a high valuation), the Company of Cathay had barely enough money to outfit the ships and hire crews for the 1577 venture. By the time the expedition returned in September that year, no funds were available to pay the wages of the miners and sailors.

The Company of Cathay, although it never obtained a royal charter, is a particularly well documented early example of a type of organization – the joint-stock company – which was in its infancy in Elizabethan times. The basic principle was simple: a group of investors pooled their money and other resources, hired men to organize and carry out an enterprise, and divided the profits in proportion to the amount that each venturer had invested. Complications arose, however, if the venture resulted in losses rather than profits. Investors were not protected from personal liability for such losses, as they are in modern incorporated organizations. Neither was the issue of additional stock or the sale of stock by an investor to someone outside the company commonly allowed as a means of raising additional financing. When new money was required to carry on a venture, the standard method for obtaining it was by assessing the existing stockholders in proportion to their investment. In enforcing such assessments, the officers of the company had only one weapon: the threat that if the additional sum was not paid, the stock would be cancelled and the venturer would lose his initial investment. The adage "in for a penny, in for a pound" aptly described the experience that investors of the period often faced, the alternative to paying up being to lose their original investment and have no hope of future return.

The first such assessment had been made to finance the 1577 expedition, when the original investors were each required to pay a sum double that which they had ventured on the first voyage. Within a few weeks of the expedition's return, they were faced with an additional investment of 20 per cent in order to pay off the crews. There next arose a need for money to finance the construction of a smelter, since Jonas Schutz insisted that only a large-scale furnace with bellows driven by water power could separate the full amount of precious metals from the difficult Baffin Island ore. In December 1577 a site was selected at Dartford, on the small river Darent, which flows into the Thames from the south, downstream from London, and the following month the venturers were informed that they had been assessed a further 20 per cent for the construction of the furnaces. Construction began in April 1578 and was well under way by the time the third expedition was launched to supply the smelter with ore.

The construction of the smelter was not the only claim on the pockets of stockholders in the Company of Cathay during the spring of 1578. In March the commissioners appointed by the Queen decided that a major mining and freighting expedition was warranted by the assays that had been carried out over the winter. They proposed that ten ships be sent to Meta Incognita, and that the outfitting of such a fleet would require an assessment of 135 per cent over the stock already invested. One can imagine the indecision of many of the stockholders when faced with such a demand. Some of the wealthier and those who had invested small initial amounts that could be lost without worry on a speculative venture probably considered it easier to pay up than be dunned by Lok or the royal commissioners. Others of the venturers who were more skeptical of the promised outcome, especially those who were members of the court or Privy Council, simply did not pay their assessments. Decisions were more difficult for the merchant investors, who lacked the security of inherited wealth and court position and whose commercial reputations depended on keeping their word. Almost all of these paid their assessments in full, but we cannot know in what combination of hope and desperation the payments were made.

The one extraordinary transaction involved Michael Lok, the treasurer of the company and original partner in the project, who sold £1,000 of his stock to the Earl of Oxford. The earl may have developed a late interest in the venture, been persuaded that he stood to profit greatly from investing, and been importunate in his desire to obtain stock. However, it is difficult to believe that Lok would have sold a major portion of his stock if he remained totally convinced of the profitable outcome of the enterprise. In the atmosphere of almost frantic haste to push events

Page from a coded letter, recently discovered and deciphered, from the Spanish ambassador in London to Philip II of Spain, reporting on the activities of a Spanish spy aboard one of Frobisher's ships (Archivo General de Simancas, leg. 831, folio 266; published by Donald Hogarth and Bernard Allaire in *Terrae Incognitae* 27 (1996): 46–57; courtesy Bernard Allaire)

forward during the spring of 1578, this transaction stands out as the first signal of doubt, the first hint that even those at the centre of the project were beginning to lose conviction.

At the same time as doubts of the commercial viability of the venture may have begun to circulate, a political element entered the picture. Dionyse Settle, one of the gentlemen who had accompanied the 1577 expedition to Baffin Island, shortly after their return produced a well-written and appealing account of the voyage and the strange new lands and peoples discovered. This small book was published in the autumn of 1577 and was quickly translated into French, Italian, German, and Latin. As well as raising English interest in the Frobisher venture, the Settle account gave credence to rumours at European courts of potentially important English discoveries in the far northwestern Atlantic. Even Ivan the Terrible, the czar of Russia, wrote to Queen Elizabeth expressing his concern over English trespassing and demanded the return of the three Inuit hostages, whom he assumed had been removed from his poorly known Siberian domains. The ambassadors of Spain and France sent confidential reports from London, as well as purloined samples of ore, which were tested and found to be without value. Spain was particularly interested in England's territorial ambitions in the New World, as well as in a potentially competitive source for the gold and silver that was largely supplied at the time by Spanish mines in Mexico and Peru. The Spanish ambassador went so far as to infiltrate a spy into the crew of the 1578 expedition, an intrigue that has recently come to light through the decoding of a document containing his report.

The English court, many of whose members were now inextricably involved in the venture, was also beginning to see the Frobisher project in political as well as economic terms. Although their motives could not yet be described as "colonial ambitions," the establishment of English sovereignty over these distant lands was now viewed by the Queen and the court as a natural outgrowth of the commercial enterprise. The orders for the 1577 voyage had included instructions to land a small number of English criminals on the coasts of Greenland and Meta Incognita, in a slapdash and ultimately unfulfilled attempt to establish an English presence. In its plans for the expedition of 1578 the court envisioned the planting of a colony of one hundred Englishmen in Meta Incognita, the first such attempt by the English in the New World.

As events accelerated during the spring of 1578, the commissioners and the venturers of the Company of Cathay juggled a variety of motives and information: the fading possibility of discovering the elusive passage to Cathay, the clouded but still lustrous hope of gaining great personal wealth from the black-ore deposits of Meta Incognita, and a growing interest in placing the English flag on a portion of the New World not yet claimed by European rivals. Although a further venture must have been against the better judgment of many investors, the project had by this time gathered an overwhelming momentum.

Ten

THE GOLD FLEET

The *Aid*, flagship of Frobisher's 1577 and 1578 voyages; detail from a painting of the battle of Smerwick Harbour by William Winter the Younger (Public Record Office, MPF 75); this is the only known representation of any of Frobisher's ships.

IN LATE MAY OF 1578 THE SMALL PORT OF HARWICH on the Essex coast saw the assembly of what would prove to be the largest fleet of ships ever sent into Arctic regions before the twentieth century. The Privy Council had decided that a mining and colonization expedition should be sent to Meta Incognita only ten weeks earlier, and the assembling and provisioning of such a fleet in this short time must be regarded as a triumph of organization. When we consider the communications capability of the period and the naval infrastructure on which the fleet could draw, Michael Lok and his associates must be credited with great competence and organizational skills. Anyone who has faced the problems of coordinating a relatively minor Arctic project over a similar period of time can only marvel that the enterprise was successfully carried out at all.

Three of the ships were veterans of the 1577 voyage: the *Aid*, the *Michael*, and the *Gabriel*; the last of these was now on its third trip to Baffin Island. Another ship, the *Judith*, had been purchased by the Company of Cathay, and six more were chartered for the voyage. In addition to these, and in possible contravention of the company's rules, Lok had personally chartered one ship and Martin Frobisher four in order to carry home private cargoes of gold ore. The fifteen ships and their captains were listed by George Best, who was himself captain of the *Anne Frances*. His list is worth reproducing, both as the cast of characters that will appear in the following chapters and as examples of the kinds of names that Elizabethans gave their ships:

The names of the Shippes with their severall Captaynes.

1 In the *Aide* being Admirall, was the Generall Captayne Frobisher
2 In the *Thomas Allen*   Viceadmirall Ca. Yorke.
3 In the *Judith*   Lieutenant General Ca. Fenton.
4 In the *Anne Frances*   Captayne Best.
5 In the *Hopewell*   Captayne Carew.
6 In the *Beare*   Captayne Filpot.
7 In the *Thomas of Ipswich*   Cap. Tanfield.
8 In the *Emanuell* [or *Armonell*] *of Exceter*   Ca. Courtney.
9 In the *Frances of Foy*   Captayne Moyles.
10 In the *Moone*   Captayne Upcot.
11 In the *Emanuall of Bridgewater* [or the *Busse*]   Ca. Newton.
12 In the *Salamon* [or *Salamander*] *of Weymouth*   ca. Randal.
13 In the *Barke Dennis* [or *Dionyse*]   Captayne Kendall.
14 In the *Gabriell*   Captayne Harvey.
15 In the *Michaell*   Captayne Kinnersley.

Lok calculated that the outfitting of the ships owned by the Company of Cathay would cost £8,363, and he neatly balanced this figure against subscriptions of £8,370, which were to be raised by the 135 per cent assessment on the stock held by investors in the company. He managed the fine balance by omitting the costs that would be due on the expedition's return, such as the wages of the mariners, miners, and soldiers and the freight costs charged for the six chartered vessels. However, the funds seem to have been adequate to hire crews on small advances against their wages and to equip and provision the ships for an Arctic voyage.

The royal commission that had been established to oversee the venture issued Frobisher with detailed instructions regarding the objectives of the voyage and how these objectives were to be attained. He was commanded to hire 90 mariners for the four ships owned by the company, 130 miners, and 50 soldiers. He was to direct his fleet to the Countess of Warwick's Island, where ore had been mined the previous summer, to find a safe harbour for the ships, to secure the island against attacks from the Inuit, and to set the miners to work. He was then to search for other deposits, assay the ores discovered, and if they proved richer than the original find, to move the ships and miners to the new locations.

The next order of business was the establishment of a settlement, and to this end Frobisher was instructed to search for a location that could be fortified against attack either by the local people or by "any other that shall seke to arryve ther from any other part of Christendom," a recognition of the political rivalry aroused in Europe by the venture. He was then to "leave to remayne and to inhabite in the lande nowe called Meta Incognita, under the charg and government of Edward Fenton, gent, your Lieutenaunte Generall, the *Gabriell*, the *Michaell*, and the *Judithe*, with fortie hable marioners, gonners, shipwrights, and carpentars, 30 soldiors and 30 pyoners, with sufficient vittalle for xviij monthes for their provisione, releife, and mayntenance, and also munition and armoure for their deefence, which nomber of persones befor specified you shall not exceed to carrie nor leve their."

The one hundred men who were to be left in Meta Incognita were to remain until the following summer, and their safety would seem to have been well considered. They were to be allowed three ships by which they could escape if no expedition returned for them and eighteen months' provisions in case they were held by ice over the first summer. Captain Edward Fenton was instructed to keep a weekly journal noting the weather, the ice conditions, and "the state of the countrie," but aside from these there were no instructions as to what the men in the settlement were to accomplish. Best informs us that the thirty miners were meant "for gathering the golde Ore togyther for the next yeare" and that the ships were to search for more potential mines. Frobisher was admonished to ensure that the men left behind took great care in their dealings with the natives and that "in all your doynges and theirs you so behave your selves and theyme, towardes the said people as maye rather procure their frindships and good lykings towardes you by courtesyes then move them to any offence or myslikings." Unfortunately, even if these instructions were followed, there was little hope of repairing the damage done to relations with the Inuit by the events of the two previous voyages.

Frobisher was instructed that, if leisure and time permitted after he had set the miners to work and planted the colony in its defensible location, he was to take the *Gabriel* and the *Michael* westwards to the location where he had lost his five sailors two summers earlier. Here he was to search, not for his men, but for more gold deposits, and to proceed 50 or 100 leagues farther west until he was certain that he had completed the Northwest Passage and entered the Pacific Ocean. He was not to continue to Cathay, however, but to return homewards with the other ships, after selecting "what place may be most aptest further to fortifye upon hereafter (yf nede requier), bothe for defence of the myners and also for possessinge of the countrie and bringe home with you a perfecte platt and parfecte notes therof to be kept in secreat, and so delyvred unto us."

The document concludes with instructions on the succession in the leadership in case Frobisher died, regulations against unauthorized persons gathering or assaying ore for their own purpose, and advice on the keeping of secure records concerning the ore and other materials collected by the expedition. Frobisher was instructed to take one or two clergymen to read divine service and administer the sacraments, to obtain information on the island of Frisland if his route took him to its coast, and to punish treason or mutiny as he saw fit.

With his instructions and authorizations in hand, Frobisher and his captains visited the court, which was sitting at Greenwich, to take their leave of the Queen. Here, according to Best's account, "they all receyved great encouragemente, and gracious countenance. Hir Highnesse, besides other good giftes, and greater promises, bestowed on the Generall a faire Cheyne of Gold, and the rest of the Captaynes kissed hir hande, tooke their leave, and departed every man towards their charge." The gold chain must have seemed an appropriate gift to the man who promised to return entire shiploads of gold to the royal treasury. We can only speculate about the nature of the "greater promises" offered by the Queen.

Having made his farewells, Frobisher assembled his ships in Harwich and on May 31 distributed to his captains a set of orders to be observed by the fleet. Most of the fifteen items covered practical matters of communication between the ships and instructions on how the captains should deal with such occurrences as fog, the discovery of land by night, or attack by enemy vessels. The first item, however, is of an altogether different nature and well illustrates the religious preoccupation of the times: "In primis, to banishe swearing, dice, and cardplaying, and filthy communication, and to serve God twice a day, with the ordinarie service, usually in Churches of England, and to cleare the glasse, according to the old order of England." This preoccupation is also apparent in the watchword to be used in challenging and identifying ships during the night: in such circumstance the challenge was to be "Before the world was God," and the reply "After God came Christe his Sonne."

Six published accounts record the experiences of the 1578 expedition, and although all tell essentially the same story, they are remarkably different in their approach, and each provides unique information. George Best, who had been Frobisher's lieutenant on the 1577 voyage, was captain of the *Anne Frances* in 1578. His accounts of both expeditions are the most complete as well as the most literate and well written, and they present Frobisher in an aura of calm heroism and efficient leadership. A very different view is given by Edward Sellman, who was Michael Lok's representative on the voyage. The Sellman journal is a bald statement of daily occurrences aboard the *Aid*, brightened by occasional disapproving accounts of Frobisher's violent arguments and other scandalous actions. Thomas Ellis, who described himself as a simple sailor, presents a brief and flowery recitation of the major events with an emphasis on storms and dangers, supplemented by a curious drawing illustrating four views of a "marvellous huge mountaine of yce" and concluding with a poem in praise of Frobisher. The journals of Christopher Hall, pilot of the *Thomas Allen*, and Edward Fenton, captain of the *Judith* and Frobisher's lieutenant on this voyage, are essentially the logs of ships' officers, with daily records of winds, tides, sailing distances, dangers from ice, and other notable occurrences. Even their reporting of activities ashore takes the form of unpolished records of daily events. Finally, the Spanish ambassador's digest of the report given by his anonymous spy aboard the *Aid* provides a bare outline of the major events of the voyage.

Frobisher and his mariners were now more confident of the location of Greenland and Meta Incognita, and they decided to follow a different and shorter route, through the English Channel and across to Dursey Head at the southwestern tip of Ireland. Somewhere off southern Ireland they encountered a small ship from Bristol that had been looted by French pirates, leaving the wounded men without food or water. Having "releived them with Surgerie and salves, to heale their hurtes, and with meate and drinke to comfort their pining hartes," the fleet sailed northwestwards into the Atlantic. The mariners noted the effects of the Gulf Stream in carrying them to the northeastwards of their course, but after only fourteen days out of sight of land they struck the coast of Greenland at the latitude of 60°, close to Cape Farewell at the southern tip of the island. As in their earlier voyages, the English still thought of this country as the Frisland of the fake Zeno map. In contrast with their experience in previous years, the ice barrier off the coast of "Frisland" did not prevent them from going ashore, and Frobisher made a landing at some point on the southwestern coast.

The occupants of the local Inuit community fled at their approach, but the English shore party looked through their tents and examined their possessions. The newcomers noted the similarity of the Greenlanders to the people of Meta Incognita and were surprised to find "a box of small nayles, and certayne redde Hearings, boordes of Fyrre tree well cutte, with dyvers other things artificially wroughte, whereby it appeareth that they have trade with some civill people." Some historians have taken these finds as evidence that the Norse communities of southwestern Greenland, which had not been heard from for over 150 years, still survived at the time of the Frobisher voyages. However, it is more likely that the nails and other articles had been obtained from more recent European voyagers, English fishermen from the Icelandic banks or Basque whalers from Labrador waters, who must have occasionally reached the Greenland coast by accident or for purposes of trade or pillage. The reports of Frobisher's discovery had the effect, however, of stimulating the Norwegian king to re-establish his rights to Greenland and bring the supposed Norse inhabitants of the country to the "right religion and form of service," by which he meant the Lutheran religion that had been established in Europe after the last known contact with Greenland.

Not knowing or caring about prior Norwegian claims to the country, Frobisher now took possession of it in the name of Queen Elizabeth and gave it the name West England. On the basis of the similarities between the Inuit of West England and those of Frobisher's Straits, the English conjectured that the two countries were joined at a higher latitude, as well as being joined to Greenland, which the Zeno map placed far to the north of its true location. Before returning to their ships, they took two of the forty dogs that they found tethered near the Inuit settlement. But mindful of their instructions, they left in payment bells, looking glasses, knives, points, and other small items.

On June 23 the fleet left the Greenland coast before an easterly wind and set out across the northern Labrador Sea, a body of water that earlier experience had taught the mariners to fear. On this crossing the usual hazards of fog and drifting ice were augmented by great herds of whales, one of which was struck by the *Salamon* while under full sail, bringing the ship to an abrupt and frightening stop. The whale "made a great and ugly noise, and caste up his body and tayle, and so went under water."

On July 2 the fleet sighted a headland that the navigators identified as Queen Elizabeth Foreland (Resolution Island) at the southern entrance to Frobisher's Straits. Happy to be so close to their destination, they sailed westwards all day through a thickening field of pack ice, until at nightfall they were within the straits. But they found "the whole place being frosen over from the one side to the other, and as it were with many walles, mountaines, and bulwarkes of yse, choaked uppe the passage, and denied us entraunce." Only 50 kilometres short of their goal, they were forced to a halt, and the following month became a time of terror for most of

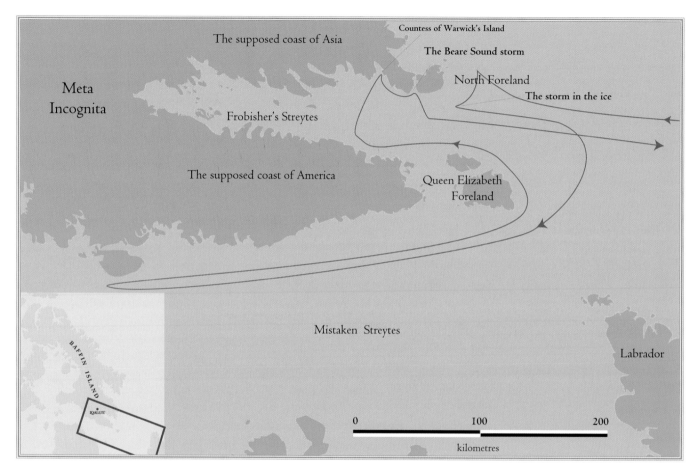

the crews. The various accounts of this period are a jumble of individual experiences. The fog was so dense that each ship lay in isolation, attempting to keep contact with the others by beating drums and blowing trumpets. Sudden winds surrounded the vessels in the crushing grip of ice, the ice-bound ships drifted towards the rocks of nearby lee shores, and the tidal currents were so swift that the roar of dangerous tide rips could be heard from a great distance.

Serious trouble began on the night of July 2, when the entire fleet had been enticed deep into the icefields at the mouth of Frobisher Bay. George Best reports that

Southern Baffin Island, showing the approximate route of Frobisher's 1578 voyage

Sea ice in Frobisher Bay during the early spring; the solid cover of ice breaks up during June and July and is flushed into Baffin Bay by winds and storms; ice begins to reform during late September and October (photo Nick Newbery).

the Fleete being thus compassed (as aforesayde) on every side with Ice, having left muche behynde them, thorow which they had passed, & finding more before them, thorow whiche it was not possible to passe, there arose a sodaine and terrible tempest at the Southeast, which blowing from the mayne Sea, directle upon the place of the straytes, brought togither al the Ise aseaborde of us, upon our backes, and thereby debarde us of turning backe to recover sea roome againe: so that being thus compassed with daunger on every side, sundrye men with sundrie devises, fought the best waye to save themselves ... And againe some were so fast shut up, and compassed in amongst an infinite number of great Countreys and Ilands of Ise, that they were fayne to submit themselves & their Ships, to the mercie of the unmercifull Ise, and strengthened the sides of their Ships with junckes of cables, beds, Mastes, planckes, and such like, which being hanged overboord, on the sides of their Shippes, mighte the better defende them from the outragious sway and strokes of the said Ise ... And yet (that whiche is more) it is faythfully and playnely to be proved, and that by many substantial witnesses, that our Shippes, even those of greatest burdens, with the meeting of contrary waves of the Sea, were heaved up betweene Islandes of Ise, a foote welneere out of the Sea, above their watermarke, having their knees and timbers within boorde, both bowed, and broken therewith.

The four rearmost ships of the convoy (*Anne Frances*, *Moone*, *Frances of Foy*, and *Gabriel*) managed to claw themselves clear of the main pack and tacked about offshore in mountainous waves and storm-tossed floes of ice, fearful that all their companions had been lost. Throughout the night, men lined the sides of the ships that were still caught in the pack, fending off ice floes with oars, pikes, and anything else that came to hand, while the mariners fought to force their way into open water. Others "soughte to save the Soule by devoute Prayer and mediation to the Almightie, thinking indeede by no other meanes possible, than by a divine Miracle, to have their deliverance." Their prayers or their efforts were so successful that only one ship was lost. The hull of the *Dennis* was torn open by the ice and she quickly sank, but nearby ships launched their boats and took off the crew before she went down. In fact, the loss of the *Dennis* turned out later to be extremely providential, since she carried to the bottom much of the timber for the prefabricated house that was to shelter the intended colonists for the following winter, men who would likely have died of cold and scurvy if they had been left in Meta Incognita.

Just before noon on July 3 the wind switched to the southwest, dispersing the ice and allowing the remaining ships to make their way to the open sea, where they joined their companions. Only the *Judith* and the *Michael*, which had become separated from the fleet and had spent the storm in the ice some distance to the north of the other ships, were still missing. July 4 was spent at sea, repairing leaks and rigging and thanking God for the deliverance of the fleet. The next day, however, the mariners found themselves in a thick fog that barely lifted for the following two weeks and would be the cause of the major navigational error which marred the 1578 expedition.

Having lost its position while getting clear of the ice and tacking about in fog for three days while attempting to stay clear, the fleet eventually sighted a distant headland which Frobisher identified as the North Foreland, at the northern entrance to Frobisher's Straits. Others were not as certain of the identification, especially since recent snow had obscured the landforms with which they were familiar. The experienced navigator Christopher Hall was convinced that Frobisher was wrong and rowed to the flagship in order to tell him so. "I told him that yt was not the Streicts, and told him all the marks of both the lands, that yt was not the Streicts, and he presently was in a great rage & sware by Gods wounds that yt was yt, or els take his life, so I see him in such a rage, I toke my pinas & came abord the Thomas Allin againe." Hall was unpersuaded by Frobisher's outburst, and he may have been unwilling to risk his ship by following what he considered to be foolish orders. In any case, the *Thomas Allen*, together with three other ships, became separated from the rest of the fleet during the foggy day of July 10 and turned back to the eastwards. It was eventually apparent that Hall had been correct: the headland that was dimly visible through snow showers and fog was not the North Foreland but Queen Elizabeth Foreland at the southern entrance to Frobisher's Straits. However, it took ten days of hazardous sailing before Frobisher and the seven other crews, who stayed with their leader, were finally convinced of his error.

With the high coast of the foreland on its starboard side, the diminished fleet steered westward into a channel obscured by heavy fog, encountering broad fields of pack ice and currents more violent than any that it had previously experienced. George Best, whose ship had joined those that abandoned the main fleet, wrote that "truly it was wonderfull to heare and see the rushling and noyse that the tydes do make in thys place with so violente a force, that oure Shippes lying ahull, were turned sometimes rounde aboute even in a momente, after the manner of a whirlpoole, and the noyse of the streame no lesse to be hearde a farre off, than the waterfall of London Bridge." For those aboard the *Aid* and its accompanying flotilla, the days passed in doubt and uncertainty. Edward Sellman appears to have had confidence in Hall's judgment of their mistake, but "The Generall and our master could not be dissuaded, but doth still make yt to be the north shore, the Generall assuring himself therof to this present (the 10th said) that yt is so, and James Beare allso, but being foggy and darkened with mystes, they cannot yet make yt perfectly, I pray God send yt clere, that we make yt perfectly."

Sellman's prayer was not answered for another week, by which time the ships were 60 leagues (180 miles or 300 kilometres) to the west of Resolution Island. On July 17 the sun finally shone from a clear sky, and the mariners could calculate their position as latitude 62°, which placed them well to the south of their previous explorations in Frobisher's Straits. By this time they were actually in the vicinity of the present-day community of Kimmirut, midway along the northern shore of the broad channel that is now known as Hudson Strait. Frobisher named it "Mistaken Straytes," and the small fleet turned about and retraced its route to the eastwards.

George Best, always inclined to be fair to his leader, stated his opinion that in fact Frobisher had realized earlier that he was in a strange body of water, but that he recognized that this channel was much more promising as a passage to the Pacific and had decided to try his luck while he had the chance. The size and nature of the Hudson Strait tides had convinced the mariners that a large body of water lay to the west. Deep within the strait they found wreckage that they took to be from the ship *Dennis*, which had sunk far to the east, convincing them that a strong westerly current flowed through the channel. Best also argued from the medieval philosophical principle that inferior bodies are governed by superior, so that water must follow the course of the heavens and move from east to west around the world, thus suggesting that the channel must be a major outlet from Atlantic to Pacific. Frobisher claimed privately that, had it not been for the call of duty, he could have sailed on through Mistaken Straits and discovered the long-sought Northwest Passage, but that he desisted from this plan in obedience to his orders. We now know that if he had continued his westward course, he would not have found the Pacific Ocean but the huge mid-continental sea known today as Hudson Bay. His navigational error lost him valuable time in his 1578 mining venture, but it was not wasted. Thirty years later Henry Hudson selected Mistaken Straits as the channel that would lead him to the bay which now bears his name and which provided the English with a route to the rich fur resources of central and western Canada.

The voyage eastwards through Mistaken Straits was as fog-ridden and perilous as the ships' entrance into the strait. Seeing a channel leading to the north, Frobisher dispatched the *Gabriel* to find out if it connected to Frobisher's Straits. The rest of the convoy continued eastwards around Queen Elizabeth Foreland, encountering additional fog, wind, and ice. Best reported that only God's merciful guidance saved the mariners from certain destruction on more than ten thousand occasions:

Manye times also by meanes of fogge and currants, being driven neare uppon the coaste, God lent us even at the very pintch one prosperous breath of winde or other, whereby to double the land, and avoyde the perill, and when that wee were all without hope of helpe, every man recommending himselfe to death, and crying out, Lorde nowe helpe or never: nowe Lorde looke downe from Heaven and save us sinners, or else oure safetie commeth too late: even then the mightie maker of Heaven, and oure mercifull God, did deliver us: so that they who have bin partakers of these daungers, do even in their soules confesse, that God even by miracle hath foughte to save them, whose name be praised evermore.

Having rounded Queen Elizabeth Foreland and made a further attempt to enter the genuine but ice-choked Frobisher's Straits, the ships began to encounter others of the fleet which had not followed them into Mistaken Straits and were also attempting to reach their port. The first was the *Anne Frances*, followed by the *Frances of Foy*, which in turn reported having met the *Gabriel*. This last ship had succeeded in passing to the west of the foreland through the channel that today is known as Gabriel Strait. The next ship met was the *Emmanuel of Bridgewater*, a large and cumbersome freighter that had been so badly damaged by ice that her crew was exhausted from manning the pumps in trying to keep it afloat.

Having come through such peril and heard from the crew of the *Emmanuel of Bridgewater* that ahead lay nothing but "Ise and Daunger," the mariners began to murmer in protest against Frobisher. Some of the officers wished to find a harbour where they could repair their ships and wait for a westerly wind that would clear the ice from the bay. Others talked of desertion, stating that they would rather be hanged at home than face inevitable death in the ice. Frobisher ignored these complaints and overcame the doubters by stating that he planned to reach port and load his ships with ore or else die in the attempt. If death in the ice became inevitable, he promised to use the fleet's supplies of gunpowder to blast and burn the ships and crews rather than let them become a prey or "spectacle" to the Inuit.

While Frobisher was fending off a potential mutiny in the icefields at the mouth of Frobisher's Straits, the *Judith* and the *Michael* had already reached their destination at the Countess of Warwick's Island. Edward Fenton spent the following ten days exploring the neighbouring islands and mainland, searching for other potential mines, and watching anxiously for the arrival of the rest of the fleet. In view of the scarce provisions on the ships, he decided to wait only until the first week of August before abandoning the venture and sailing home. On July 23 he took twenty-six soldiers on a march of approximately fifteen kilometres into the high rolling country to the north of the Countess of Warwick Sound. From a hilltop at the furthest point of his trek, he identified Gabriel Island and could see far up Frobisher's Straits, but had no sight of the other ships. Fenton makes no mention of raising a cairn or other marker at this location, but such an activity would have been typical of English sailors investigating new territory. Three centuries later the Frobisher Bay Inuit spoke of a monument that had been raised long ago by *qadlunaat* in this area and where the Inuit left gifts in hope of gaining luck in hunting caribou. The location of such a marker is not currently known, but one may have been raised on this warm July day by Fenton's soldiers. The warmth of the day is suggested by his note that on their return they had to cross a major stream, which was much larger than it had been that morning and had sufficient water to power two mills. I have shared with Fenton and his companions the experience of long-distance walking on a warm Arctic summer day, when streams that in the morning were ankle-high trickles are by late afternoon impassable waist-deep torrents fed by melting snow from south-facing valleys.

Fenton also inspected the equipment and stores that had been left from the previous summer. The men found that a pinnace they had sunk for retrieval the next summer had apparently been scuttled in water which was too shallow and had been destroyed by the ice. The mast-step from the pinnace and the remains of a barrel were discovered in an abandoned Inuit camp. Fenton's party also found "divers osmondes which we lefte uncovered lying in their places untooched of the people." The term "osmonde" was applied at the time to small ingots of high-quality iron that were used as raw materials for blacksmithing. Such objects would have been of inestimable value to the Inuit, who had a long history of working with metal as intractable as the meteoric iron of northwestern Greenland. Iron ingots would undoubtedly have been removed by them, for cutting and hammering into blades for arrows, harpoons, and knives. The fact that these osmondes were untouched (and on another occasion similar osmondes had been moved but abandoned by the Inuit) suggests that they were objects of another description and were in fact the iron blooms — lumps of low-grade iron and slag weighing about ten kilograms — which have led to a good deal of puzzlement among the archaeologists who found them in association with the Frobisher sites.

While Fenton searched for additional ore deposits, the rest of the fleet was scattered along the southern shore of Frobisher's Straits fighting heavy ice, contrary winds, and snow. George Best reports that "In this storme, being the sixe and twentith of July, there fell so much snow, with such bitter cold ayre, that wee could not scarce see one another for the same, nor open oure eies to handle our ropes and sayles, the snow being above halfe a foote deepe uppon the hatches of oure shippe, which did so wette thorowe our poore Marriners clothes, that he that hadde five or six shifte of apparrell, had scarce one drie threede to his backe, whiche kinde of wette and coldenesse, togither with the over-labouring of the poore menne amiddest the Ise, bred no small sickenesse amongst the Fleete." The sailors must have had some respite a few days later, for just after describing the snowstorm, Best noted that "the Sunne many times hath a marvellous force of heate amongst those mountaines, insomuche, that when there is no breth of winde to bring ye cold ayre from ye dispersed Ice uppon us, we shall be weary of the bloming heate."

By July 30 some of the ships had worked their way to within rowing distance of the Countess of Warwick Sound. Frobisher finally reached his destination in a small pinnace and joined Fenton aboard the *Judith*. Mariners from the *Judith* and the *Michael* were sent out to the rest of the fleet as local pilots, and over the coming days the other ships were brought safely, if not undamaged, into the sound by their fright-ened and weary crews. The first objective of the summer — to reach the gold deposits — had cost the expedition two months of hardship and anxiety. Their ships safely anchored off the Countess of Warwick's Island, the men were led by the min-ister Thomas Wolfall in the first English service of thanksgiving in the New World. The preacher "made unto them a godly Sermon, exhorting them especially to be thankefull to God for theyr strange and miraculous deliverance in those so danger-ous places, and putting them in mynde of the uncertainetie of mans life, willed them to make themselves always ready, as resolute men, to enjoy and accept thanke-fully whatsoever adventure his devine Providence should appoynt." (Best's account of the 1578 voyage).

Eleven

THE COUNTESS OF
WARWICK'S ISLAND

I FIRST SAW THE COUNTESS OF WARWICK'S ISLAND on an August day in 1990, 412 years after the summer when Frobisher had used it as his headquarters. We had left Iqaluit, at the head of Frobisher Bay, in the early morning, and for an hour the throbbing helicopter flew southeastwards over a landscape of tundra-covered hills rolling to a coast of steep bluffs and rocky shoals. Scattered veils of falling snow obscured the landscape, and as we cleared the final flurry, the island suddenly lay before us, a small and almost circular scrap of rock barely rising above the grey sea. As we banked around the coast, the remains of Frobisher's mines emerged as great scars in the landscape, while groups of boulders marked the locations of English tent camps, caches, and other structures. We landed on a flat patch of gravel, unloaded our camping gear, and climbed to the top of the island as the sound of the helicopter faded into the northwest. For the next few days of brilliant sunshine I was privileged to experience the island as a historical document, a place where the remains of ancient events lay undisturbed and seemingly unchanged since the English fleet had slipped away in an autumn storm over four centuries ago. All the leading players in the Frobisher drama had also walked about this tiny island during the summer of 1578, scanning the surrounding waters for the sails of missing ships or the kayaks of Inuit visitors, huddling in the shelter of boulders from wind-driven sleet, and sleeping in dripping tents pitched on the hard gravel. Simply experiencing the island as it is today brings to life the sketchy journals and workaday accounts of daily life written during that distant August.

Early August on Baffin Island brings a perceptible seasonal change. Autumn colours begin to tinge the tundra vegetation, the hordes of July mosquitoes are diminished

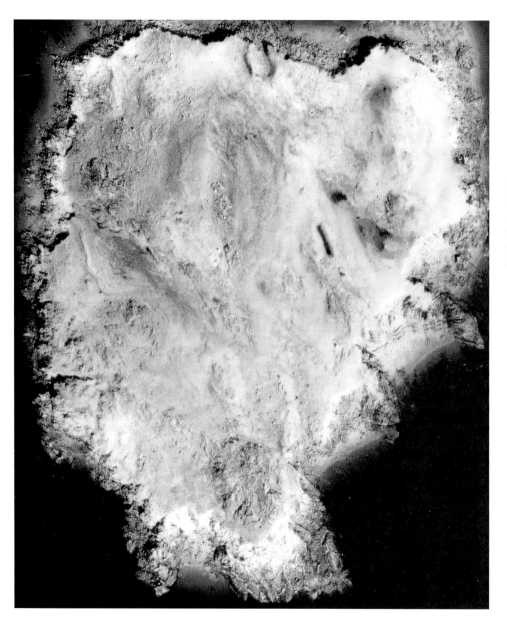

Aerial photograph of the Countess of Warwick's Island, now known by its Inuit name Kodlunarn Island; the remains of Frobisher's mines are clearly visible (National Air Photo Library, Ottawa).

Detail from a model of the Countess of Warwick's Island showing ships loading in the summer of 1578 (Canadian Museum of Civilization; photo Steven Darby)

by overnight frosts, and flurries of snow start to replace the rain showers of the previous month. The summer of 1578 seems to have been particularly cool, judging from the accounts of severe ice conditions and July snowfalls; so by the first week of August the approach of winter must have been easily felt. From their experience of previous years, the English knew that they had a very few weeks before sea ice would begin to form around their ships, and the storms of autumn would increase the hazards of a transatlantic voyage with heavily laden ships. Yet by early August fourteen ships lay empty of cargo; not a ton of ore had been loaded, nor had any provision been made for the colony that was to be left behind in Meta Incognita.

On August 1 Frobisher led a large work party ashore on the Countess of Warwick's Island, where the men cleared off the mines that had been begun the previous summer and began to set up camp for the miners and soldiers. The miners were set to work digging ore, and the mariners began discharging ballast from their ships. They must also have established a small assay furnace, for Fenton notes in his journal that that evening they made the first assays of ore.

The following day a muster of all the men was called on the island, and with the sound of a trumpet, a set of orders was proclaimed covering a mixture of commercial, sanitary, and other practical concerns:

1 no person was to go ashore except on the Countess of Warwick's Island and the adjacent island named Winter's Furnace without permission, nor was anyone to engage in any dealings with the natives;

2 no person was to make assays of ore except those authorized by Frobisher, nor was any rock or other commodity to be collected as private property;

3 no ship was to load ore without Frobisher's permission;

4 all the captains were to assemble three days hence at four o'clock in the morning to decide on the loading of the ships;

5 no person, on sea or land was to engage in swearing, brawling, or cursing, on pain of imprisonment;

6 no person was to draw a weapon, on pain of losing his right hand;

7 no person was to wash his hands or anything else in the spring of water on the Countess of Warwick's Island, and all were to relieve themselves on the beach below the high-tide line, on pain of imprisonment for fourteen hours for a first offence and a fine thereafter; and

8 no captain was to allow the discharge of ballast or other rubbish where it would impede the loading of the ships.

With these rules promulgated and understood by all, the company was set to work. As we saw in an earlier chapter, the mine that had been dug the previous year was located at the northern end of the Countess of Warwick's Island, and when finished, it formed a ramp through the sea cliffs providing access to the surface of the island. In 1578 the miners appear to have searched for a continuation of the same vein of rock and found either a low outcrop or a deposit close to the gravel surface about a hundred metres to the southeast of the first mine. They may also have been attracted to this locality by a group of three huge black boulders that lie on the surface in line with the strike of the first ore vein. Interestingly, the position is purely

View from the top of the mine that cuts through the cliffs at the northern end of the Countess of Warwick's Island (photo Walter Kenyon)

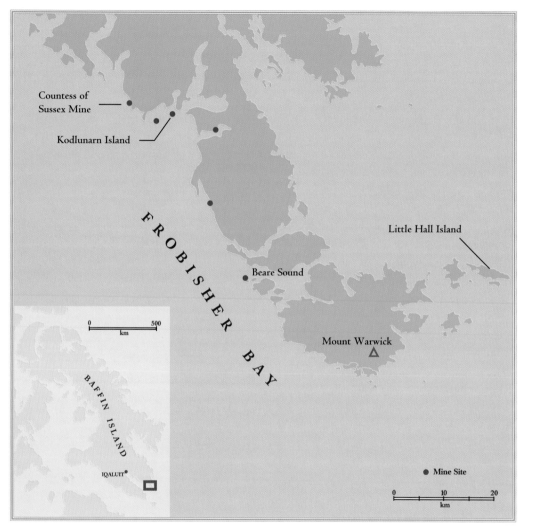

Outer Frobisher Bay, showing the site of mines that have been identified by archaeologists and other locations

coincidental since these boulders are of an unrelated type of rock and seem to have been dropped at their present position by glacial ice.

The remains of the mine that was opened on the island surface in 1578 now lie as a shallow trench about 25 metres long, 5 metres wide, and 2 metres deep. Most of the work here was accomplished during the first week after arrival, for it soon became apparent that the rock was harder than expected and more difficult to mine. Edward Sellman's accounts list only 65 tons of ore taken from the Countess of Warwick's Island this year, and the disappointing results led to a search for other deposits where ore was more plentiful, or at least easier to mine. Sellman, summarizing the summer's activities, expressed his concerns regarding this development: "Forasmuch as the Countesse of Warwick myne fayled being so hard stone to breke and by judgement yielded not above a hundred tunnes, we were driven to seke mynes as above named and having but a short tyme to tarry and some proofs made of the best owr fownd in those mynes above-said, men were willed to get their lading of them and every man so employed him self to have lading, that many symple men (I judge) toke good and bad together: so that amongst the fleets lading I think much bad owr will be found."

Frobisher and the other officers set off in small boat parties to search for more profitable deposits, and the samples with which they returned were tested by the five assayers brought for that purpose. The chief assayer, Robert Denham, supervised the establishment of an assay furnace on the Countess of Warwick's Island, which now became the command centre rather than the mining centre for the expedition. Temporary furnaces were also set up at other locations, and it is clear that several samples from a variety of mine sites were processed, and the results were used in selecting which ore to mine and load into the ships. The usefulness of these field assays is questionable, in view of the later findings that none of the ore returned to England contained significant quantities of precious metal.

One of the first locations searched was Jonas' Mount, where in 1577 the assayer Jonas Schutz had located rock that he thought to be very rich in gold. Edward Fenton began to search for this locality in late July, before the other ships had arrived in the Countess of Warwick Sound, but the deposit could not be rediscovered

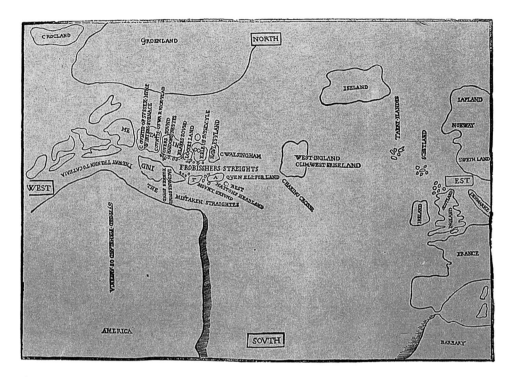

This map of the Arctic marking the location of several of Frobisher's mine sites is attributed to James Beare, principal surveyor with the 1578 voyage (from Stefansson and McCaskill 1938; photo Harry Foster).

despite the fact that Fenton had visited it in 1577 and one of the assayers had been hired particularly because he had been there with Schutz the year before. The lack of easily mined ore on the Countess of Warwick's Island was the second major disappointment of the expedition, yet hopes remained high that the black rocks found at several other localities would prove as rich.

On August 2 Frobisher took two pinnaces to Beare Sound, located 9 leagues (40 kilometres) to the southeast of the Countess of Warwick's Island, where several tons of rock had been mined the previous summer and left to be loaded the following year. The first assays were made that evening on several samples that had been brought back from Beare Sound, and their results encouraged the development of this location as one of the largest mine sites excavated in 1578. The following day Frobisher and Fenton visited a site that had been located the previous summer on a nearby island and given the name Winter's Furnace. Here they faced another

Most of the industrial activity on the Countess of Warwick's Island took place in this small valley, which contains the remains of two or more small structures (Canadian Museum of Civilization; photo Robert McGhee).

disappointment, since Fenton reported that the deposits were "founde to lie so uncertainlie and crabbedlie to gett, as we founde smale hoope of anie good there."

On August 4 Frobisher made another unsuccessful search for the elusive Jonas' Mount, and the following day he and Fenton visited a location that they called Fenton's Fortune, located a few kilometres to the southeast on the Baffin Island coast. Here they found what they considered a "greate store of oare" and reported that 1,000 tons could be mined at this site. On August 9 most of the miners were moved from the Countess of Warwick's Island to this new location, but Robert Denham now reported that with very heavy labour they would get barely 40 tons. It finally turned out that only 5 tons of ore were loaded from Fenton's Fortune. Miners were also transported farther down the coast to the previously located Beare Sound location, where an estimated 430 tons of ore were mined over the following three weeks.

Fenton notes that on August 11 he and the assayer Denham set off to investigate a deposit that had been discovered on the Baffin Island coast, a few kilometres to the northwest of the Countess of Warwick's Island. Denham had assayed the ore and found it as rich as that from other localities, and they were impressed by the amount of black rock that was available at this site. Accordingly, men were set to work clearing the overburden from what was called the Countess of Sussex mine, which was to provide 455 tons of ore, the largest amount taken from any of the Frobisher mines.

The prosaic reports of daily travel in tiny, overcrowded boats only occasionally betray the dangers that the seamen and miners faced from sudden winds, swirling tidal currents, and frigid Arctic waters. One revealing account is found in Fenton's journal for August 7.

Thursdaie the viith daie. In the morninge the winde was at est and by north and blew verie much winde. The Generall notwithstanding with Capten Randoll and Capten Courtney departed in their pynnasses with divers pyoners and soldiours to fentons fortune to gett oare there, and I following with a new pynnas called the Serche with fyve or six and thirtie pyoners in her, had not sailed from the Countesse Ilande above one mile and a half, but I bare my maste and sailes over borde, in casting abowte to meete the

The second mine on the Countess of Warwick's Island (Canadian Museum of Civilization; photo Robert McGhee)

Generall, who was forced by the extreemitie of the winde to reatorne back againe, and Capten Courtney with his companie in great daunger of drowninge, who in the night dreamed he was sinking in the sea, and so troubled therwith in his sleepe, that he cried with such lowdnes, Jesus have mercie upon me, that we in the other tents were awaked therwith and mistrusting a larom, issued owt to understande the cawse.

Even when they were safely ashore, life was neither easy nor comfortable for the mariners, soldiers, and miners. Fenton continues his account of August 7 by stating that, having been turned back by the wind, "we were forced eftsones to ymploie our souldiours and pyoners in the Myne on the Countesse Ilande, notwithstanding abowt 4 of the clock in the afternoone it began to Raine and the winds contynewed at est blowing all the night extreemelie with much Raine."

In mid-August the air temperature in southern Baffin Island hovers within a very few degrees of freezing. Calm days are rare, and the frequent showers of rain, drizzle, sleet, and wet snow are driven by winds from which shelter cannot be found among the treeless hills. Tent canvas is soon saturated and leaking, clothing and sleeping bags sodden. Today, as in Elizabethan times, fuel is too scarce to be used for warming tents or drying clothes. In 1578 the highlight of a miner's day would have been the few minutes standing near a cooking fire, wolfing down pease porridge or salt beef and hard bread, swilled down with cold sour beer. The rest of the day would have been back-breaking labour, splitting and carrying awkward blocks of stone, or shivering in wet clothes on a gravel mattress beneath a sagging and often dripping tent. The perpetual cold wind, the rumble of waves on the nearby beach, the barren cloud-capped hills extending to an infinite distance and visible all through the twilit nights, and the fear of surprise by outlandish and ferocious natives were all constant elements of life on the Countess of Warwick's Island. In view of the adversity and discomfort of their lives, we can barely credit the amount of work that was accomplished by Frobisher's crews during the month of August 1578, and much of the credit must go to Frobisher and his officers, who – contrary to later British naval tradition – laboured as hard as the men. According to George Best, "whylest the Mariners plyed their work, ye Captaines sought out new Mynes, the Goldfiners made tryall of the Ore, the Marriners discharged their shippes, the Gentlemen for example sake laboured hartily, and honestlye encouraged the inferiour sorte to worke. So that small time of that little leasure, that was lefte to tarrie, was spent in vaine."

Mining was not the only activity ordered by the commissioners who had drawn up Frobisher's instructions. The establishment of a colony in Meta Incognita, under the leadership of Edward Fenton, remained a priority, and on August 9 Frobisher called a counsel of his captains to discuss the viability of this project. They began by examining the bills of lading from each ship, in order to determine the whereabouts of the various parts of the prefabricated building that was to house the colony. This survey yielded the information that only the southern and eastern walls of the structure were on ships currently at the island. Much of the remainder had been on the bark *Dennis*, which the previous month had sunk in the ice off eastern Baffin Island. Other portions were on the *Moone*, the *Anne Frances*, or the *Thomas of*

Ipswich, which had last been seen off Queen Elizabeth Foreland before the fleet entered Frobisher's Straits. Even the parts of the structure which had arrived had suffered considerable damage when they were used as fenders during the fleet's adventures in the ice.

As important as the lack of shelter was the lack of beer, which was considered an essential food for the men who were to be left behind. The three missing ships carried eighty-four tons of beer, which had been meant for the wintering party, and Fenton considered that the twenty-four tons of beer that remained was clearly insufficient. He nevertheless volunteered to winter on the Countess of Warwick's Island with a smaller number of men, but the carpenters claimed that there was only enough timber to build quarters for forty men, and that the building could not be erected in less than eight or nine weeks. Since such a delay would have meant an Atlantic crossing during the season of November storms (or the very real probability of the ships being frozen in for the winter in Frobisher Bay), Frobisher decided to abandon the proposed colony. We can imagine the relief with which this decision must have been greeted by many of the men who had been assigned to remain after the fleet set sail for home.

While the main portion of the fleet was shuttling around the Countess of Warwick Sound on the north shore of Frobisher Bay, the *Moone*, the *Anne Frances*, and the *Thomas of Ipswich* had been caught in the ice at the southern entrance to the bay and were unable to follow the other ships to their intended port. George Best had effective charge of this small flotilla, which was soon reduced to two ships when the crew of the *Thomas of Ipswich*, deciding that they had seen enough ice and dangerous weather, forced their captain to slip away in the night and head homeward to England. The *Anne Frances* and the *Moone* had both suffered damage from being crushed in the ice and needed a local harbour in which to make temporary repairs, yet the mariners were wary of the rocky shoals and tidal currents of inshore waters and the possibility of having their vessels frozen in. Best set out in the ship's boat to reconnoitre a harbour and somewhere in the vicinity of the present-day Resolution Island found "a great blacke Iland, wherunto he had good liking." The black rock which composed the island appeared to be the same as that brought home the previous summer from the Countess of Warwick's Island. He named this island Best's Bless-ing, on the assumption that if the ore proved to be as rich as that from the other side of Frobisher's Straits, "it was to be thoughte that it might reasonably suffise all the golde gluttons of the worlde."

The two ships were brought into the neighbouring bay, but in the process the *Anne Frances* was holed by a rock and only saved by desperate pumping before the leak could be stopped. While the ships were being repaired, the miners began load-ing over two hundred tons of rock, and the carpenters attempted to build a pinnace that Best could use to cross to the Countess of Warwick's Island in order to search for the rest of the expedition. After their terrible experiences in the ice, the men aboard the *Moone* and the *Anne Frances* suspected that they might be the only survivors of the entire fleet. Best also planned to use his pinnace to search the coasts to the west, "where by if any of the Fleete hadde been distressed by wracke of rocke or Ise, by that meanes they might be perceived of them, and so they thereby to give them such helpe and reliefe as they could. They did greatly feare, and ever suspecte that some of the Fleete were surely caste awaye, & driven to seeke sowre sallets amongst the colde cliffes."

The carpenter of the *Anne Frances* was at a great disadvantage, since he found that some vital parts of the prefabricated pinnace were missing; nor were there any nails to hold the planks together. The carpenters remedied the latter deficiency by break-ing up tongs, gridirons, and fire-shovels to obtain iron from which they could forge nails, using a gun chamber as an anvil and a miner's pickaxe as a blacksmith's ham-mer. The contraption was finally assembled and floated on 18 August, and Best pre-pared to set out, against the advice of the ship's carpenter, "who saide that he would not adventure himselfe therein, for five hundred poundes, for that the boate hung togither but onelye by the strength of the nayles, and lacked some of hir principall knees and tymbers."

The following day Best embarked, accompanied by the captain of the *Moone* and eighteen volunteers, among whom we may assume the wise carpenter was not included. Not wishing to venture a direct crossing of Frobisher Bay, they rowed westward for 40 leagues (200 kilometres) up the steep and fjord-indented southern shore. Here the channel narrows to the point where a crossing of 20 kilometres would bring them to a series of islands in the middle of the bay. The crossing was "not a little daungerous" and was barely accomplished when a sudden storm drove the mariners among the shoals and forced them to land at night on Gabriel Island, the large island that had been named for Frobisher's bark in 1576.

Before we follow the rest of their journey, it may be worthwhile taking a small diversion. Best notes in his journal that at the place where they landed on Gabriel Island, "they did find certaine great stones sette uppe by the Countrie people, as it seemed for markes." In his edited version of the journal, the Arctic explorer Vilhjalmur Stefansson notes, "These would be slabs or long stones up-ended for caribou driving." And indeed, throughout the Inuit world such monoliths were commonly used to construct drift fences for directing the movement of caribou or to mark the locations of food caches, trails, or other features. Best's men, however, added to the local architecture by setting up "manye Crosses of stone, in token that Christians had bin there." It is tempting to suggest that these stone crosses were the original models from which developed an icon of Eastern Arctic Inuit culture: the piled-stone figure known as an inukshuk, which has recently been chosen as the central feature of the flag adopted by the Territory of Nunavut.

In the Inuktitut language, *inuksuk* means "like a man," and these stone figures that watch over many Eastern Arctic landscapes are usually thought of as "stone men." However, their usual form – a small cairn or vertically placed boulder supporting a large horizontally placed slab and topped by a central stone "head" – could equally well be interpreted as a cross. Although simple stone markers or cairns have always been used by Arctic cultures to mark location or direction, this specific form appears to have a relatively recent history. The human-like or cross-like inukshuk is not found in the regions occupied by the Inuit of the Central and Western Arctic. None are known in the High Arctic regions, which the Inuit inhabited until the fifteenth or sixteenth centuries. In fact, the distribution of this particular structure is centred in southern Baffin Island and along the coasts of Hudson Strait and northern Hudson Bay. These were the coasts explored by Frobisher, Hudson, and the various seventeenth- and eighteenth-century European venturers who preceded the whalers into Hudson Bay. As we know from the Frobisher and later accounts, the Inuit inhabiting these coasts were eager to attract Europeans ashore in order to trade for metal; those whom Frobisher encountered showed themselves atop hills, waving flags, and shouting in order to bring themselves to the attention of passing ships. The piled-stone figures standing along these coasts may have had a similar function, as permanent markers informing visitors of the presence of potential trading partners. If so, the knowledge that Englishmen assigned significance to boulders piled in a cruciform structure may have led to the development of what has become an iconic Arctic figure.

Having spent the night of August 21 and built their field of stone crosses on Gabriel Island, Best and his men continued their journey eastwards along the northern shore of Frobisher Bay. They had sailed about forty kilometers when they spotted smoke, tents, and people waving a flag. Assuming that the group on the shore were natives, the boat party approached with caution lest they be attacked: "They haled one another according to the manner of the Sea, and demaunded what cheare: & either partie answered ye other, that all was well: wheruppon there was a sodaine and joyfull outeshoote, with greate flinging up of cappes, and a brave voly of shotte to welcome one an other. And truelye it was a moste straunge case, to see howe joyfull and gladde everye partie was to see themselves meete in safetie againe, after so straunge and incredible daungers: Yet to be shorte, as their daungers were greate, so their God was greater."

The men turned out to be the crew under Captain York who were working the newly discovered Countess of Sussex mine, located 10 kilometres to the northwest of Frobisher's headquarters on the Countess of Warwick's Island. After greeting the companions whom both parties had given up for lost and exchanging news, Best and his men continued southeastwards and soon arrived at the Countess of Warwick's Island. The first order of business was assaying the samples of rock that they had brought from the Resolution Island mine known as Best's Blessing. Robert Denham made six tests which showed that the ore contained both silver and gold, and Best reported that it "proved to be very good." He was accordingly ordered to return to his ships, load them with ore from Best's Blessing, and rejoin the rest of the expedition. On August 24 he set out, in what we hope was a more securely constructed pinnace, to recross Frobisher Bay.

The number of assays carried out on the ore that Best brought to the Countess of Warwick's Island (two on the evening of August 22 and four the following day) suggests the frequency with which this operation could be undertaken under what must have been primitive conditions. We may ask if these were the same sort of complete assays that had been done in London during the previous winter or an abbreviated form adapted to the field situation. Fire assaying involved crushing a sample of ore, placing it in a ceramic crucible, and melting the ore in a furnace, then mixing in molten lead to alloy with the precious metals. After cooling, the crucible was broken to reveal a small "button" of lead which was heated in a "cupel" made from bone ash, a material that absorbed the lead in the form of oxides and left a small bead of gold and silver. There is archaeological evidence that at least one and probably two small temporary shelters on the Countess of Warwick's Island were used as assaying workshops. The scattered remains of charcoal, broken crucibles encrusted with slag, cupels, and other refractory ceramics indicate that the standard techniques of fire assaying must have been carried out here. Donald Hogarth, a geologist who has studied the mining and metallurgy of the Frobisher voyages, suggests that a simpler form of assaying may also have been practised: simply roasting the black ore in a furnace and testing it with nitric acid. Heating the black rocks of the outer Frobisher Bay area oxidizes their high mica content to a golden colour. While working on the Countess of Warwick's Island, modern researchers used a simple camp stove to heat small chunks of rock and easily obtained the same effect; a black rock became golden brown, a change that to an eager and willing mind might possibly seem to be evidence of precious metal. Standard fire assaying is a long and complicated process, and if short cuts such as this were used, they might account for some of the mistaken results that encouraged the miners in their futile tasks of digging rock and loading it aboard their ships.

Best reached his ships on August 25, and finding them fully loaded and ready to sail, he returned to Frobisher's headquarters after dropping off his miners to help with the work at the Beare Sound mine. For the first time since the early July storm in Davis Strait the entire surviving fleet was now together in one place, and it was time to finish the work and head for home before the expedition was assailed by the storms and newly formed ice of autumn. Several tasks had to be undertaken during the final week of August. Frobisher had not been successful in several attempts to capture Inuit hostages, and now he took a pinnace to Gabriel Island, where he hoped to find people at the settlement that Best's party had discovered there. His reason for wishing to capture native hostages is not clear; it may have been a final effort to recover the men whom he had lost two summers earlier, or he may have wanted to collect people who could be trained as interpreters for use in future dealings with the Inuit. Whatever the case, the Inuit avoided capture on this as on previous occasions when they had appeared in the neighbourhood of the mines, confident in their ability to paddle their kayaks more swiftly than the English could row their heavy boats.

While Frobisher was away searching for hostages, and supervising the loading of ore at various mine sites, Fenton was left in charge of preparations for leaving the Countess of Warwick's Island. The provisions that had been brought to support the intended hundred-man colony, as well as the remnants of the prefabricated barracks, were buried in the mine at the northern end of the island in the hope that the material would be preserved for use if the expedition returned for more ore in coming years. It was at this point that George Best, in what must have been an unusually optimistic mood observed, "Also here we sowed pease, corne, and other graine, to prove the fruitfulnesse of the soyle against the next yeare."

Fenton also set the masons and carpenters to work at the summit of the island, building a structure that he referred to as a watchtower. Best reports of August 30:

This daye the Masons finished a house which Captaine Fenton caused to be made of lyme and stone upon the Countesse of Warwickes Ilande, to the ende we mighte pruve againste the nexte yere, whether the snowe coulde overwhelme it, the frosts breake uppe, or the people dismember the same. And the better to allure those brutish and uncivill people to courtesie, againste other times of oure comming, we left theirin dyvers of oure countryie toyes, as belles, and knives, wherein they specially delight, one for the necessarie use, and the other for the great pleasure thereof. Also pictures of men and women in

Model of the Countess of Warwick's Island as it may have appeared during late August 1578, when timber and supplies were cached in the mine at the northern end of the island (Canadian Museum of Civilization; photo Steven Darby)

lead, men a horsebacke, lookinglasses, whistles, and pipes. Also in the house was made an oven, and breade lefte baked therin, for them to see and taste.

This small structure, the remains of which can still be seen on the summit of the island, constitutes the first recorded house built by the English in the New World.

On the same day that the house was completed, the *Anne Frances* was hauled ashore in order to repair the many leaks that had remained unmended from her adventures with ice and rocks, which must have been worrisome to a crew setting out on a transatlantic journey. We do not know where this careening took place, but in view of the local situation and later Inuit stories about a ship having been built here, the trench formed in the cliffs by the mine at the northern end of the Countess of War-wick's Island seems a likely location. The tides in outer Frobisher Bay run to ten metres or more, and August 30 was only two days away from the new moon, so the tides would have been more extreme than usual. This condition would have facilitated the beaching and repair of a ship, and indeed, for periods of several hours at a time this trench would have been a convenient natural slipway, while the timbers that were being buried in the mine at the time would have provided plenty of material for temporary skids and props.

A final duty was undertaken before the expedition left the relative security of the Countess of Warwick Sound for the open Atlantic: "Maister Wolfall on Winters Fornace preached a godly Sermon, whiche being ended, he celebrated also a Communion upon the lande, at the partaking whereof was the Capitaine of the *Anne Fraunces*, and manye other Gentlemen & Soldiors, Marriners, & Miners wyth hym. The celebration of divine mistery was ye first signe, seale & confirmation of Christes name death & passion ever knowen in all these quarters." (Best's account of the 1578 voyage). Sermons were preached and Communion celebrated on several of the ships as well, so that all the scattered company could participate.

Frobisher then called together the captains and consulted with them as to whether it would be possible to undertake a further search for a Northwest Passage, in conformity with the instructions given him by the royal commissioners before the voyage began. Best reports that the captains willingly volunteered to carry out such an enterprise, but that it

was found a thing verye impossible … especially for these causes followying. First, the darke foggy mistes, the continuall fallyng Snowe and stormy weather which they commonly were vexed with, and nowe dayly ever more and more increased, have no small argument of the Winters drawing neare. And also the froste everye nighte was so hardly congealed within the sounde, that if by evill happe they shoulde be shutte uppe there faste the whole yeare, whyche being utterly unprovided, woulde be their utter destruction. Againe, drincke was so scant throughout al the Fleete, by meanes of the greate leakage … al the way homewards they dranke nothing but water.

In view of the deteriorating weather conditions, it must have required little debate to decide that the time had come to leave for home. We may also suspect that there was heated discussion about the "great leakage" of beer, which according to Best had been caused by loading coal and timber on top of the barrels. Edward Fenton's journal for this day records that the greatest wastage of beer was on Best's own ship, which had carried the bulk of the supplies meant for use by the wintering colony. Fenton suggested that the wastage came, not from "evill casking," but from negligence and abuse among the crew of the *Anne Frances*, "whose loosenesse of behaviour in this accion hath been well discovered, but sloolie punnished," and he probably made this view known at the council of captains.

Whatever the mood of the council, the decision to forgo additional exploration and immediately depart for England was certainly wise, and it was taken none too soon. Frobisher distributed a set of articles for the Atlantic crossing: the captains were ordered to keep company with the fleet, not to remove any ore from the ships without permission, to turn in all rock samples or other souvenirs taken from either Meta Incognita or West England (Greenland), and to return all mining gear after they reached home. Most notably, if any ship was separated from the fleet and captured by an enemy vessel, the captain was to cast into the sea all maps, logs, and other material that might provide information as to the location of the new land and its gold mines. The orders having been distributed, most of the ships fully loaded, and all other duties accomplished, on September 1 the fleet began its voyage homeward.

Twelve

RETREAT

THE LAST SHIPS OF THE FLEET SAILED AWAY from the Countess of Warwick's Island on September 1 and gathered off the Beare Sound mine about thirty kilometres to the south. Here Frobisher was supervising the effort to load a final cargo of ore aboard the *Gabriel* and the *Michael*, as well as on the large freighter *Emmanuel of Bridgewater*. By the evening a northwesterly wind was rising, and not wishing to be caught on a lee shore during the coming storm, the captains who could do so raised their anchors and sailed for open water, planning to rendezvous off Queen Elizabeth Foreland. Some ships had left their miners ashore at Beare Sound, creating a dangerous situation for the remaining vessels, which had neither the accommodation nor the provisions to carry the men to England. The apparent panic of the following days contrasts with the competence with which perilous circumstances had been handled throughout the summer. Edward Sellman, who was aboard the *Aid* tacking about offshore in dangerous seas waiting for Frobisher, stated that "the Generall is condemned of all men for bringing the flete in danger to anker there, thwart of Beares Sound only for 2 boates of owre and in daungering him self allso, whom they judge will hardly recover to come aboord of us, but rather forced to go with the barks or the Emanuel of Bridgewater into England … Master Hall went aland after the ship came first to an anker thwart the said Bears Sound, and did geve him counsaill to make hast a boord before night: God send him well to recover us and his company." As usual, Hall's advice was both excellent and unheeded.

On the morning of September 2 Fenton reported "much winde at north northwest with some snow and sleete." He recovered the *Judith*'s anchor and set sail for Queen Elizabeth Foreland, but the storm was so severe that it sank the ship's boat before the crew could get the boat aboard, as well as a pinnace that was being towed. George Best had left his ship, the *Anne Frances*, the previous evening and joined Frobisher aboard the *Emmanuel* in order to supervise the distribution of men. By morning the storm was so much worse and the *Emmanuel* in such a desperate situation that Frobisher and Best abandoned the freighter and her crew. As many men as possible were transferred to the tiny *Gabriel* and *Michael*, and each ship also towed a pinnace packed with miners. Best escaped with about thirty men in his rickety pinnace towed astern of the *Michael*. Very fortunately, the *Anne Frances* had waited for her captain a few miles offshore, for as soon as the men had clambered aboard the ship, their pinnace "sheavered and fel in peeces, and sunke at the ships sterne, with al the poore mens furniture."

The storm that blew during the crossing of Frobisher Bay on September 2 seems to have been as severe as anything experienced during the three years of Arctic voyaging. Best reported that "in this storme, manye of the fleete were daungerously distressed, and were severed almost al asunder. And there were lost in the whole Fleete well neere xx. boates and Pinnesses in this storme, and some men stroken over boorde into the sea, and utterly lost. Manye also spente their mayne yardes and mastes, and with the continuall frostes, and deawe, the roapes of our shippes were nowe growen so rotten, that they went all asunder." That evening Frobisher cast loose the pinnace that was being towed by the *Gabriel* and instructed the men to go aboard the larger ship *Moone*. The captain of that ship, apparently not wishing to provide for more men than he already had aboard, set full sail with the pinnace in hazardous pursuit. The *Moone* escaped, and the fortunate men seem to have been those whom Edward Sellman reports as having been in a pinnace picked up by the *Aid*.

By September 3 the fleet was scattering before a strong northwesterly gale, setting its course to the southwards so as to avoid the Greenland coast and reach warmer waters as quickly as possible. Frobisher had tried to find the *Aid*, but having missed her, he was making the crossing once again in the *Gabriel*, the small bark that had first carried him northwestwards two summers earlier. The most complete account of the return across the Atlantic comes from the journal of Sellman aboard the *Aid*, whose duties as accountant now allowed him more time to note matters aboard ship.

His ship had left Resolution Island in company with two others, but in a storm on the night of September 5 the crew lost sight of the *Moone*. In the middle of the night of September 10 their main yard broke, and despite the fact that they fired a cannon and put out signal lights, their remaining companion, the *Thomas Allen*, continued on her way and by morning was out of sight. A few days later a wave from astern swept through Frobisher's cabin on the *Aid*. Frobisher himself was still aboard the *Gabriel*, but the record books containing all the information on assays undertaken on Baffin Island, which were kept in the cabin, were washed overboard. On the 19th of the month the ships were in latitude 51°, about the latitude of Bristol and in the warmer waters of the North Atlantic Drift, when they sighted three sails that they suspected were those of warships. Cautiously approaching the nearest ship, they discovered her to be the *Anne Frances*, and they took aboard several men for whom the smaller ship could not provide. They also learned of the problems encountered at Beare Sound and of the fate of the *Emmanuel*, which had last been seen anchored among rocks on a lee shore. Sellman wrote, "God send good news of her, she was left in great perill." No accusation was recorded that Frobisher had abandoned the ship and her crew, but there can have been little doubt that this was the case. As many men as possible had been taken off by the *Gabriel* and the *Michael*, but the rest of the *Emmanuel*'s crew had been left behind in what appeared to be a hopeless situation.

Against all odds, however, the *Emmanuel* had in fact found a way out of her danger. Unable to break free from the coast of Beare Sound in the face of the continuing northwesterly gale, the crew had discovered a narrow and dangerous channel leading eastwards from the bottom of the sound. Now known as Lupton Channel, this rock-filled and current-swept strait separates the large island of Loks Land from Baffin Island. With what must have been a combination of great skill and luck, the unwieldy *Emmanuel* made the passage safely and emerged into Davis Strait, where the captain set his course for England. The adventures of the *Emmanuel* had barely begun, and an eventful crossing was in store. On September 8 the ship passed the southern tip of Greenland. Four days later and approximately 250 kilometres to the southeast the crew sighted a large and previously unknown island which they named the Island of Buss after their ship (the *Emmanuel* was a Dutch type of vessel known as a "bus" or "busse," and she was often referred to in the journals under the name the *Buss of Bridgewater*). According to the report of a passenger, the Island of Buss was so large that the *Emmanuel* sailed along its coast for three days. George Best reported that he had been told it was "seeming to be fruitful, full of woods, and a champion countrie." The only other reported sighting of this island occurred a century later when it was described by Thomas Sheperd, and on the basis of his reports *The English Pilot* began to map it as a diamond-shaped island with a range of mountains up the western coast, rolling hills in the east, and several named headlands, bays, and harbours. Not until the nineteenth century was it removed from English maps, at a time when the North Atlantic was so extensively known that the island's existence could no longer be believed. It is still not clear whether the crew of the *Emmanuel* mistook an extensive field of ice and fog for an island or whether the entire account was fabricated out of whole cloth.

On September 25 the *Emmanuel* made land about midway down the west coast of Ireland, but her luck had finally run out. For the following six weeks, battered by storms and contrary winds, the ship beat up and down the Irish coast but was unable to make any headway towards England. Eventually she was driven into the bay of Smerwick, at the outer end of the Dingle Peninsula, "withowte masts, sailes, boate, ancre or any other convenient furniture." Here she was beached as a derelict, but Captain Richard Newton took care to protect her cargo of ore. One hundred tons of rock were carried ashore and stored in a "fort," probably a farm building, on a headland above Smerwick Harbour, where two men were left as guards while the rest of the crew continued home to England. There Newton, who was the owner as well as the captain of the ship, petitioned the Privy Council and was granted the ore as recompense for the loss of his ship. However, by the time this agreement was made, in the spring of the following year, the true value of the ore had become apparent and the owner did not bother to collect his property.

The Baffin Island ore did find a local use in Ireland, however, when the following summer a band of Spanish, French, and Italian soldiers under the rebel James Fitzmaurice made a landing at Smerwick and fortified the headland where the ore had been stored. The fortification was enlarged in 1580 in order to protect a bigger party of Spanish invaders. The *Aid* was one of the ships that the English sent to put the fortress under siege, and it is to a painting of the battle of Smerwick Harbour that we owe the only known image of one of Frobisher's ships. The blockade soon resulted in the fall of the fort and the massacre of over five hundred of the occupying soldiers and allies. When geologist Donald Hogarth visited the site in 1988, blocks of black Baffin Island rock were coming loose from the fort and falling to the beach below. Having been quarried from the western shores of the North Atlantic, been transported at great risk across an ocean, and witnessed one of the more brutal incidents in Irish history, the black Baffin Island rocks are now returning to the sea.

By the time the *Emmanuel* was abandoned in Ireland, the rest of the fleet had reached England safely, having passed through the English Channel and arrived in the Thames around the beginning of October. The summer had taken its toll on the strength and health of the crews, however, and Edward Sellman's account of the voyage home is a litany of deaths. Scurvy must have been setting in, and there is little doubt that a few more weeks of service would have witnessed a decimation of the miners, mariners, and others involved in the enterprise. As it was, Best was able to bring his narrative of the journey to a conclusion with the statement "There dyed in the whole Fleete in all this voyage not above fortie persons, whiche number is not great, considering howe many ships were in the Fleete, and how strange fortunes wee passed." The adventuring phase of the Frobisher episode was complete. Now came the time for assaying and accounting and eventually for the apportioning of blame over a venture that would soon be universally regarded as an unmitigated failure.

Thirteen

DISGRACE

MOST OF THE ONE THOUSAND TONS OF BAFFIN ISLAND rock that survived the Atlantic crossing eventually made its way to Dartford, the tiny mill town downstream from London that had been selected as the site for the smelters built to refine gold from Frobisher's ore. Jonas Schutz had convinced the royal commission that the full measure of gold could be removed from the ore only through the use of such massive industrial machinery, and construction had been going forward throughout the summer of 1578.

The scale of the enterprise is suggested by just a few items in the detailed accounts of construction that have been assembled by James McDermott from the account books of Michael Lok and others engaged in the project. Purchases included more than 300 tons of squared oak timbers, over 20,000 bricks, and over 40,000 roof tiles. The complex was described in one report as comprising "two great workhousses, & two watter mylles, with fyve great meltinge furnaces in the same housses, & one great Colehous, & other necessarye workhouses." The water wheels were used to drive the ten giant bellows that provided blasts of air required to smelt ore, and the proper placing of these bellows was a continuing cause of dissension between Schutz, who had designed the furnaces, and his detractors.

Trains of horse-drawn carts transported over fifteen hundred loads of ore up the muddy autumn roads from shipside at the Thames to Dartford, and smelting trials continued through the winter of 1578–79. Several furnace loads of ore were smelted in the first five months after the ships returned, but the procedures and the results were poorly reported. This was almost certainly a consequence of the meagre results of these trials, none of which produced the promised quantities of sil-

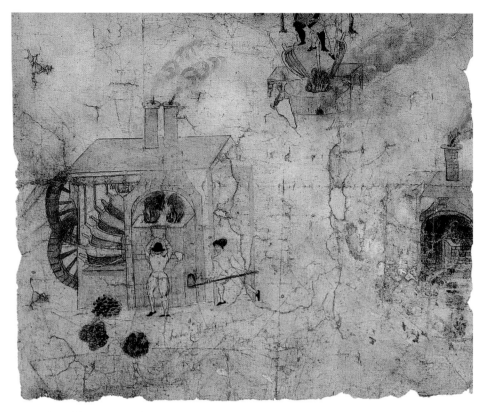

The smelting furnaces at Dartford, as depicted by an unidentified artist (Public Record Office, MPF 304)

ver and gold. Two trials were reported on November 13, one as "verye evill" on account of the additive that was used and the other as "somewhat reasonable," but on these results "the Ewre brought back by Captain Furbisher grewe into great discredit." A trial reported on December 29 "succeeded but evill." A final attempt was made on February 17, which produced a tiny amount of gold but 35 ounces of silver per ton. This outcome was not promising, since the process had used a lead-ore additive that was known to contain silver and was probably the source of most of the metal that resulted from the test.

Given their poor understanding of the processes involved in smelting and refining metals, some investors blamed these results on the design of the Dartford furnaces, the nature of the additives, or Jonas Schutz's lack of ability as a metallurgist.

By February 1579, however, there was a widening realization that the ores were worthless. The best evidence of this development comes from a report to the king of Spain, written on February 7 by Don Bernardino de Mendoza, the Spanish ambassador in London, as quoted by historian Robert Baldwin.

As I have had no safe opportunity until now I have not previously sent the chart about which I wrote on 15 November, when speaking of Frobisher's voyage. I now forward it with specimens of all kinds of ore brought. They are but of little value as the Englishmen and assayers confess, and no matter what heat is employed they cannot smelt them satisfactorily, owing to their great crudity which is a certain sign that they are not rich. To remedy this, it occurred to the Germans who were managing it that it would be advantageous to mix the ore with powdered pyrites, of which they ordered a cargo from Plymouth. This proves conclusively that the assays last year were exaggerated to increase the fame of the business. It is not thought of much now for the sailors have not been paid and the merchants who took shares in it have failed, so that people are undeceived.

Each week of the winter must have added to the burdens facing members of the Company of Cathay. As each smelting trial produced only further news of failure, debts from the construction at Dartford added to those already accumulated from the third voyage to Baffin Island. Shipowners had not been compensated for freighting the ore to England; miners and mariners remained unpaid. The court was demanding results and requiring proof of the ores' value, "for that her Majestie hathe very great expectation of the same." An additional assessment of 85 per cent of their previous investment was levied on the stockholders of the company in order to maintain solvency, an assessment that the officers found difficult to collect.

By this time the tensions and mistrust between various groups of venturers were beginning to break into the open. Animosities that had developed during the 1578 voyage itself, notably between Frobisher and officers such as Fenton and Hall, were now openly expressed. The most conspicuous split was between the group aligned with Michael Lok and the assayer Jonas Schutz and those aligned with Martin Frobisher. In the spring of 1578 Frobisher had expressed his distrust of Schutz and had backed Burchard Kranich's assays as providing the proofs that made the third voyage possible. Schutz had won the contract to design and supervise the Dartford smelters, and by November 1578 Kranich was dead, but the ill-will between Lok and Frobisher was not healed. Despite having survived an audit of his accounts during the summer, Lok was removed from his post as secretary to the Company of Cathay before the end of 1578.

This situation led to the creation of a remarkable document, written by Lok and entitled "The Abuses of Captayn Furbusher Agaynst the Companye, Ano 1578." Its curious mixture of serious charges and unsubstantiated malice gives the document an almost humorous tone, which nevertheless fails to conceal the desperation of a man fighting for his reputation and financial survival. Such a testament is difficult to summarize, but its importance makes the attempt worthwhile:

- "No.1: The ewr promysed was not brought." In the first voyage Frobisher had brought home by chance a stone from Little Hall Island which was rich ore and had "said that in that countrie was inoughe therof to lade all the Quenes shippes, and promised to lade the shippes of the seconde voiage ther withall." However, on the second voyage he had found no more ore where the first had come from and had "laded the ships with other mynes founde by chaunse."
- "No.2: The ewr promised was not brought." On the second voyage Frobisher also discovered, by chance, red and yellow ore from Jonas' Mount, which Burchard Kranich found to be rich in gold. He promised the commissioners "that ther was mountaynes therof, and he would lade all the shippes therwithal in the thirde voiage." However, during the third voyage the expedition was unable to rediscover this source, and he "brought home not one stoane therof."
- "No.3: Superfluous shippes and charges. He carried 4 ships and c. men without comission." For the third voyage Frobisher hired four extra ships and a hundred men on his own account, in order to bring home a larger quantity of ore, "which he said was better then the best that was brought the yeare befor, which is not yt so found." His additional ore was proving worthless, and the costs for these ships and men had now been charged against the company.

- "No.4: He would not place C. Fenton there." Frobisher was against the plan to settle the hundred-man colony under Captain Edward Fenton and refused to assist him, "feringe that C. Fentons deede therin woulde dashe his glorye, and because he toke the victualls of that provision to victuall his own 4 shippes taken with him extraordinare."
- "No.5: He made no discovrie of passage." Although instructed in 1578 to send the *Gabriel* and the *Michael* on further explorations for the Northwest Passage, Frobisher did nothing, "but made all his endevour to lade his owne shippes, and the rest home agayne with ewre."
- "No.6: His owne men evell officers in the shippes." Frobisher was prodigal in outfitting the ships for the 1578 voyage, and the men whom he appointed officers "made verie great spoile, wast, and pilfrye of the goods in the shippes."
- "No.7: He mayntayned D. Burcott's doings." This item refers to events during the spring of 1578, when Frobisher chose to support the optimistic assay results of Burchard Kranich over those of Jonas Schutz.
- "No.8: He vittelled the shipe *Aide*." Frobisher was sent to Bristol with funds to provision the *Aid* for the 1578 voyage, but although he was to purchase enough meat for four meals per week, he bought only enough for two or three meals a week, and for the rest he substituted "evill fishe, and that with scarsetie wherbye manye of them died, as the men do reporte."
- "No.9: He dealt doble in the miners provision." Similarly, the company had provided funds to hire 120 West Country miners. However, Frobisher is reported to have coerced local communities to provide miners at their own expense, with the result that many provided "showmakeres, taylores, and other artificers, no workmen."
- "No.10: He toke the shippe Salomon by commission." While still in the West Country, Frobisher had coerced the owner of the *Salomon* to provision his ship at his own expense and provide it for the 1578 voyage, against promised payment that he did not make.
- "No.11: He led the flete of ships to wrong place." This accusation refers to Frobisher's dangerous venture into the ice of Frobisher's Straits and the later excur-

sion into the Mistaken Straits, "wherby they were all in great danger to perrishe, as Hawll, Davis and the rest of the shipps masters will witnes."

- "No.12: He denied the Councells comission." While in Meta Incognita, Frobisher had refused to comply with the Privy Council's instructions, claiming that they were forgeries prepared by Fenton and Lok.
- "No.13: He caused the great disorder of the ships retorne home." This item refers to the confusion and near-disaster that occurred when the storm of September 1 hit the fleet, which Frobisher had ordered to the unprotected coast of Beare Sound. Curiously, even in this document he is not criticized for abandoning the crew of the *Emmanuel* to almost certain death.
- "No.14: His arrogancie." The witness of Hall, Jackman, Davis, and the other captains of the 1578 voyage is called as testimony to Frobisher's arrogance and to the fact that the captains, as well as some of the commisioners and many of the venturers in the company, are "mynded to medle no more with him."
- "No.15: He drew his dagar on Jonas." This allegation refers to the incident in February 1578 when Frobisher threatened to kill Jonas Schutz if he did not complete his assay in time for the third voyage to be organized.
- "No.16: He drew his dagear on C. Fenton." On another occasion at Dartford, probably in the fall of 1578, Frobisher had made a similar threat to Edward Fenton.
- "No.17: Litle trewthe in his talke … He is so full of lyinge talke as no man maye credit anye thinge that he doth speake, and so impudent of his tonge as his best frindes are most sclanndered of him, when he cannot have his wille."
- "No.18: He sclandered M. Lok, to the great domage of the Companye." Frobisher had made loud and false allegations regarding financial irregularities in Michael Lok's administration of the company.
- "No.19: He paid wages to men against comaundment." Frobisher had paid the crew of the *Thomas of Ipswich* almost twice as much as had been agreed by the commission.
- "No.20: He brought men into wage without order." Frobisher had hired more men, and at higher wages, than had been agreed.
- "No.21: The men in the *Aide* make great spoyle." Frobisher was still supporting a

disorderly crew of men whom he had placed on the *Aid* while at harbour in the Thames.

- "No.22: He hath not distributed the ^cli to the men." At the return of the 1577 voyage the Queen had given Frobisher as reward £100 to be distributed among the men, but he had kept it for himself.

- "No.23: To conclude, yf his doinges in thes iii voyages be well looked into, parchanse he wilbe found the most unproffitable sarvante of all that have sarved the Companye therin."

This extensive list of charges provides clear insight into the emotions and personal ill-will that had developed among those involved in the Baffin Island venture as it began to unravel. Frobisher wasted no time and little effort in replying to these charges. His response is preserved under the title "The Sclanderous Clamors of Captaine Furbusher Against Michael Lok. 1578" – "He hathe made false accountts to the Companye, and hathe cossened them of iii ^mli of money. He hathe cossened my Lorde of Oxford of ^mli. He hathe not one grote of venture in these voiages. He is a bankerot knave." Frobisher's statement that Lok had ventured no money on the voyages was patently untrue, and in fact he lost more than most other investors in the Company of Cathay. Certainly, he appears to have been the only person involved who went to prison as a debtor, and he was one of the few who discharged most of his debts. By the calculations of the official auditors, who in the spring of 1581 were assigned by the Privy Council to examine the books of the derelict company, Lok had invested £2,180, of which only £27 remained outstanding. Nevertheless, as treasurer of the company until replaced in late 1578, he bore the brunt of the investors' anger. Neither his reputation nor his finances recovered from the Frobisher episode, in which he had involved himself with such uncharacteristic enthusiasm.

The fate of the other venturers and their debts is not as fully known. James McDermott has calculated that the entire three-year episode cost almost £25,000, of which about £18,000 had been raised from the assessment of stockholders and £2,000 recovered from the sale of equipment, leaving a deficit of about £5,000 outstanding at the end of the enterprise. The official auditors made negative comments about most of those involved in the financial aspects of the venture, and as McDermott reports, "If anyone came out of the enterprise with their reputations enhanced, we have yet to discover any evidence of it."

Hope dies hard in mining ventures, and some investors remained convinced that the fault lay in the smelting process rather than in the ore itself. In 1580 an attempt was made to test the Dartford smelters by processing copper and lead ore of known composition. The attempt was not as successful as had been hoped, and the assayers noted that "in the smeltinge of the sayde roasted yewres we founde suche wante in the buildinge of the furnace and the disorderlye placinge of the bellowes that we coulde not by anymeanes possible perfectlye smelte downe all the sayde yewres but muche therof remayned in the furnace and was turned into a great lumpe commonlye termed a sowe." Such reports must have raised the hopes of those who still believed the Baffin Island ores to have value. The following winter, as part of his negotiations to be relieved of his debts and avoid debtor's prison, Lok made an unsuccessful offer to buy the entire consignment at a price of £5 per ton . However, by this time the general view of the ore's value is witnessed by the fact that large quantities were used in the construction of a wall bounding the Queen's Manor House near the smelting works. Boulders of black Baffin Island rock can be seen today in the wall bordering Priory Road in Dartford, a visible legacy of the venture that once centred on this small town in the Thames valley.

The final attempt to wring value from the ore was made in 1583, using Sir William Winter's London furnace, which had produced some of the assays on which the venture was established. The trial was a failure, but few had expected or hoped for anything more. The central figures in the venture had by this time adapted to circumstances in a variety of ways. Michael Lok had secured his release from debtor's prison and was attempting with little success to rebuild his fortune. Edward Fenton continued his involvement in both mining ventures and naval exploration, and in the latter he was joined by the competent navigator Christopher Hall. Robert Denham had success in several mining-related activities, but his erstwhile superior, Jonas Schutz, receded into obscurity. John Dee left England for central Europe in 1583, probably in large part because of the financial embarrassment over the Frobisher

This stone wall surrounding the Queen's Manor House in Dartford, England, incorporates many boulders of black Baffin Island rock brought to England by Frobisher (Canadian Museum of Civilization; photo Robert McGhee).

venture. He had convinced himself that Edward Kelly, who served as Dee's medium in contacting angels and other spirits, also had access to the philosopher's stone, which was capable of changing base metal into gold. That one motive for this journey may have been the hope of wealth through alchemical means available in central Europe reveals some measure of the low level of chemical and metallurgical knowledge that characterized even the most erudite minds involved in the Frobisher venture.

Martin Frobisher himself spent the first years after the return from Baffin Island defending himself against those who had charged him with financial swindling in his dealings related to the voyages. Some of the accusations that were made by Lok were corroborated by others, and it seems likely that Frobisher was vulnerable to such claims. Biographer James McDermott sums up the situation with his characteristically clear-eyed view of Frobisher's character. "The accusation [of misusing funds in victualling the ships] is hardly implausible: a man with a record of piracy against his own countrymen could not be thought incapable of petty theft, particularly where personal financial circumstances forced his hand. In the months following the return of the third voyage, it seems that Frobisher's most pressing problem – even allowing for the collapse of his reputation – was money ... Frobisher's financial position therefore made him subject to temptations, which he might otherwise have resisted, though his former career inclines us to think it unlikely that he would ever have been entirely unmoved by the opportunity."

In the following years Frobisher was given several small commissions from the Queen, including the 1580 blockade of Smerwick Harbour. Whether he actually arrived at that event is in question, but if he did, he would have had the opportunity to view the wreck of the *Emmanuel*, which he had last seen in desperate circumstances off the coast of Baffin Island. In 1582 he was appointed to lead a major trading and raiding voyage to the Pacific, but was removed from its command before the expedition sailed and was in fact replaced by Fenton. Sir Francis Drake appointed Frobisher vice admiral of his 1585–86 voyage to raid Spanish colonies in the Caribbean, and on his return from the expedition Frobisher purchased a manor at Altofts near his ancestral home in Yorkshire. The source of funds for this purchase is not apparent, leading to suspicions that he renewed his privateering activities during these years. His reputation changed remarkably in July 1588 when he commanded the *Triumph*, at a thousand tons the largest ship in the English navy during the battle against the Spanish Armada. Frobisher was a vice admiral of the fleet and was knighted for his valuable service, but he quarrelled violently with Drake, whom he accused of taking more than his share of both the glory and the spoils. The early 1590s were a period of obscurity for Frobisher, but it has been suggested that the several properties he acquired during this time were purchased with the spoils of successful and profitable privateering.

Martin Frobisher's final service to the Queen was made in 1594, when he led the successful assault on a Spanish fortress in Brittany. During the battle he was wounded by a musket ball, and he died two weeks later after reaching Plymouth. It was the fate to be expected of a man whose entire life was characterized by impetuous action, unquestioning bravery, and the willingness to lead by his own example. He had taken the same sort of action eighteen years earlier when the bark *Gabriel* was foundering in the northwestern Atlantic, an action that saved the ship and opened the way for one of the most remarkable episodes in the history of Arctic North America.

Fourteen

KODLUNARN ISLAND

FOR CENTURIES BEFORE MARTIN FROBISHER ARRIVED, the Baffin Island Inuit must have encountered occasional wooden ships crewed by the people whom they called *qadlunaat*, the people with big eyebrows. The earliest *qadlunaat* would have been Greenlandic Norse, but they had more recently been replaced by Basques, Portuguese, English, and Bretons. Both Inuit and Europeans would have been attracted by curiosity and by the opportunity to engage in a trade which was mutually profitable and could be carried out in safety between groups that were roughly equal in numbers and weaponry. The first reaction of the Inuit to Frobisher's visit in 1576 shows that a wary trading etiquette had been developed between the Inuit and European sailors. Yet nothing in their history would have prepared the Inuit for the invasion by fifteen ships and several hundred men. Despite the valuable goods they possessed and their apparent willingness to trade, these *qadlunaat* had been violent and dangerous neighbours, with a penchant for shooting at people and trying to capture them for some unknown purpose.

Now the *qadlunaat* had abandoned their island headquarters, leaving behind great quantities of wood and other valuable materials, which they had buried in one of their mysterious trenches. Within days, probably within hours, the Inuit would have ventured to the island and begun to assess the horde that had fallen into their hands. For people of a treeless country, accustomed to using whale bones and scarce drift-logs for the many things that other peoples made from wood, the great cache of oak boards and timbers which had been meant for Edward Fenton's winter barracks would have been a massive treasure. Next in value would have been the nails used in building the flimsy workshops and constructing the roof of the small watchtower

The archaeological excavation of Inuit winter villages near Kodlunarn Island recovered Frobisher material that had probably been salvaged from the Countess of Warwick's Island (photo Anne Henshaw).

that Fenton had erected at the island's summit. The bells, knives, mirrors, whistles, and pipes that had been placed in the watchtower would have quickly found new owners and would soon have begun to pass along the widespread trade network which linked the local Inuit group to others throughout Baffin Island and beyond. Eight years later the explorer John Davis went ashore in Cumberland Sound, about two hundred kilometres to the north, and found an Inuit sled "made of firre, spruse and oaken boards sawn like inch boords." We can be fairly certain that these boards originated with the construction materials buried by Frobisher on the Countess of Warwick's Island. A second and more profitable phase of mining had begun on this small island, which in the process had acquired a new name: Qadlunaat or White Man's Island.

While the Inuit preserved traditions related to the people who had left the valuable materials on Qadlunaat Island, the locations of Frobisher's explorations and mining endeavours were soon lost to the knowledge of Europeans. In 1595, a year after his death, Gerhard Mercator published an updated version of his Arctic map which showed Frobisher's Straits as a narrow channel behind the southern tip of Greenland. Various other locations were suggested over the following centuries, but until the 1860s the location of Frobisher's mines remained a mystery. The rediscovery came about through a much later and more disastrous episode in the search for a Northwest Passage. By the mid-nineteenth century the formidable barriers to Arctic transportation were widely recognized. Merchants and politicians had largely abandoned the idea of a commercial shipping route, yet the discovery of a northern passage from Atlantic to Pacific remained a grail for geographers and naval officers. In the 1840s the British Navy decided that one final push would break open the Passage, and it equipped the largest expedition sent to the Arctic since Frobisher's. Under the leadership of Sir John Franklin, two ships and 135 men disappeared into the channels of the Arctic archipelago in the summer of 1845 and were never seen again.

Rescue efforts were mounted when no news of the expedition had been received by 1848, and they continued through the 1850s, although it was clear that the three years of provisions would long since have been exhausted, and hope for the men's survival gradually died. Franklin's first winter camp was found, then a message hidden in a cairn reporting events up to the spring of 1848, when the icebound ships had been abandoned, and finally a sad trail of human skeletons and discarded possessions leading southwards towards the Arctic mainland. The ships themselves have never been located.

Into this picture in 1860 came the American journalist Charles Francis Hall, who thought it possible that some of the men from the Franklin expedition might still survive by living with Inuit groups. He raised funds for a personal expedition and got a berth on the New England whaling ship *George Henry*, sailing for the eastern coast of Baffin Island. Here he met the Inuit who worked with the whalers and began to learn their language and how to travel with them by sled and whaleboat. Baffin Island was far to the east of the Central Arctic region where the Franklin expedition had disappeared, but Hall had hopes of making an excursion westward after he had become a competent Arctic traveller and had hired reliable Inuit guides. In the meantime he joined a party of Inuit travelling into Frobisher Bay, both as a training exercise and in the hope of carrying out some local exploration.

Hall was a prolific writer, maintaining a variety of journals, logs, and diaries in a series of small bound books, which today reside in a cabinet at the Smithsonian Institution's Armed Forces History Collections. Turning the water-stained pages and attempting to decipher the cramped writing in smudged black ink, I found it difficult to conceive the discipline and will required to write several hundred words every day under the conditions of nineteenth-century Arctic travel. After I had become accustomed to reading the misspelled but spare and vivid prose of Eliza-bethan adventurers, Hall's florid and self-conscious Victorian style, even in these rough journals, felt like wading through syrup. His published account of naming the small river that flows into the head of Frobisher Bay is copied directly from one such diary: "Now beside a noble river. Its waters are pure as crystal. From this river

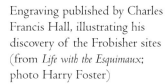

Engraving published by Charles Francis Hall, illustrating his discovery of the Frobisher sites (from *Life with the Esquimaux*; photo Harry Foster)

1861
Aug
11

my feeling were. Any how, I was all —
all heart.

The subject of this heart seema
sea-Coal of Frobisher's Expedition
of 1578! — Near three Centuries
Ago??

Koo-ou-le-arng, seeing that I had discovered
something that made me (corn water dancing?)
joyous, came running with
all her might. Though she & other Innuits have
known all about this coal being here (as I find by
what she & Koo-jis-se inform me to-night) yet
not a word had ever been communicated to me
about it. I had heard of brick & heavy Stone (the latter of
course, I thought to mean iron), but nothing of Coal's.

Soon as Koo-ou-le-arng came up, I held out
hand to her, wh was full of coal, asking:

Kis-u ? (what is this ?)

She answered; "Innuits Kook-um". By this I took
it that the Innuits sometimes have used it in cooking
Said I: Innuit Ik-ku-men ? An-me-larng (yes)
was the instant response. I then asked: Now-kma?
meaning, Whence did these coals come from?

Koo-ou-le-arng's response was: Kod-lu-nam
Ki-ete umalnable echan ? — A great many years ago White
men with big Ship came here.

This answer made me still more joyous.
From what I find Koo-ou-le-arng had com-

1861 / 3d me
Aug
11 / 3d day
out

municated to her friends Innuits
some of my Conduct while on that coal
pile wh. I discovered this morning:

She said that I acted just like an Ange-Ko
that I done one thing an Innuit couldn't do — that I had
danced & laughed — & made a complete
somerset on the Coal! — This much I may
record; if I really danced, & accomplished the latter
feat, as she declares I did, I have done what I
never did before in all my life!

However, I am not reluctant to acknowledge the truth
in all its simplicity for "veritas nihil veretur nisi"
abscondi. Truth is afraid of nothing but concealment.
I felt like dancing — like turning a dozen of somersets!

And why did I feel so happy?

Because of the
discovery I made to-day of what is a Confirmation of
the testimony — oral history — I had acquired
great perseverance from the Innuits. That a great many
years ago — many generations age — Kod-lu-nark
Oo-mi-ark-chu-a (White men with big
ships) came into this Bay (Kin-nut-joke-ping-
oo-sy-ong) — because of the chain that I felt
was now complete the determined this to be the
Bay that Frobisher discovered in 1576 & revisited conse-
cutively in the years 1577, 1578 — & that Ni-oun-te-like
the Island of my visitation to-day was the identical one
on wh. Frobisher landed with the object of establishing
Winter quarters for the Colony of 100 men that he
brought here in his last voyage, in 1578!

The account wh. Frobisher gave of his discovery
was indefinite that the civilized World has remained in
doubt where it is as to its location. Even to this day It anywhere
know not its location. Some one has made a
guess & approximated to the fact — simply approximated.

In a few days I trust I shall return, then confirming it to be

I have taken a draught on eating by its banks American cheese and American bread. The American flag floats flauntingly over it as the music of its waters seems to be 'Yankee Doodle.' I see not why this river should not have an American name. Its waters are an emblem of purity. I know of no fitter name to bestow upon it than that of the daughter of my generous, esteemed friend, Henry Grinnell. I therefore, with the flag of my country in one hand, my other in the limpid stream, denominate it 'Sylvia Grinnell River.'"

While he travelled in Frobisher Bay, Hall's Inuit companions told him stories about five *qadlunaat* who had been marooned in the area, had lived with the Inuit over a winter, and had then built a ship and sailed away. He was also told about *qadlunaat* who came to the area in several ships, constructed a stone house, dug a trench as a reservoir on a small island, and built a ship there. The island was named after the *qadlunaat*, a name that Hall transcribed as "Kodlunarn Island," which is the name it retains on current maps. At first he thought that he had found clues to the missing Franklin expedition, but the geographical location was wrong and the stories related to events that had occurred far longer ago than the fifteen years since Franklin was last seen. Eventually he concluded that the oral traditions of the Inuit referred to an episode that had taken place almost three centuries earlier, the Frobisher expeditions to what was then known as Frobisher's Straits.

Hall persuaded his guides to take him to the group of islands where these events had occurred, and the journal entry for August 11, 1861, reports his search for a black rock that he had seen from a distance:

I was now nearing the spot where I had first descried the black object. It again met my view; and my original thought on first seeing it resumed at once the ascendancy in my mind. I hastened to the spot. "Great God! Thou hast rewarded me in my search!" was the sentiment that came overwhelmingly into my thankful soul. On casting my eyes all around, seeing and feeling the character ("moss-aged," for some of the pieces I saw had pellicules of black moss on them) of the relics before and under me, I felt as — I cannot tell what my feelings were. What I saw before me was the sea-coal of Frobisher's expedition of 1578, left here near three centuries ago!

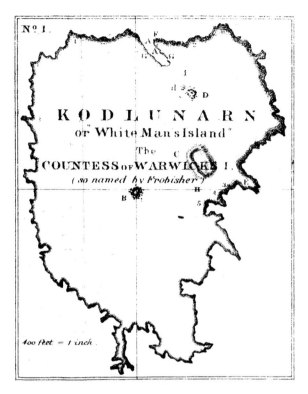

Charles Francis Hall drew this remarkably accurate map of Kodlunarn Island and the Frobisher remains he discovered there (from *Life with the Esquimaux*; photo Harry Foster).

The following month, on his return from the head of Frobisher Bay, Hall was taken to nearby Kodlunarn Island, where he was shown the two large mine trenches and the ruins of Fenton's hilltop watchtower. These remains indicated that Kodlunarn Island was none other than Frobisher's Countess of Warwick's Island, the head-quarters for the 1577 and 1578 expeditions. Hall collected fragments of pottery, brick, roof tile, flint, and coal, as well as a large loaf-like chunk of iron that he thought to be a "proof" left over from the activities of Frobisher's assayers. This material was bundled into his old stockings, and when he returned to the United States in 1862, the specimens were divided between the Smithsonian Institution in Washington and the Royal Geographical Society of London.

Charles Francis Hall did not return to Baffin Island but continued his Arctic adventures in other regions. From 1865 to 1869 he travelled in the area where

Inuit drawing of the monument left by the English and tended by generations of Inuit; see page 110 (from *Life with the Esquimaux* by Charles Francis Hall; photo Harry Foster)

Franklin had disappeared, discovering more relics of the lost expedition. In 1871 he was commissioned to lead a polar expedition aboard the ship *Polaris*, but he died during the first winter in northern Greenland. In his prolific journals Hall claimed that he was being poisoned by the ship's doctor. A 1968 autopsy on his frozen body, recovered from its permafrost grave, proved that his suspicions had been correct.

Hall's amateur archaeology, guided by the traditions of the Inuit, had discovered the sites of Frobisher's activities after their location had been lost to European knowledge for almost three centuries. Despite its historical interest, Kodlunarn Island and the nearby mine sites have until recently been protected by their isolation from most visitors and souvenir hunters. The first competent archaeologist to visit the island was Walter Kenyon, from the Royal Ontario Museum, who undertook a brief documentation and carried out further excavations at the watchtower in 1974, as well as searching for and locating several of the related mine sites. Kenyon reported his work in a fine book titled *Tokens of Possession*, which combines a summary of the Frobisher story with a characteristically breezy narrative of Kenyon's own experiences in pursuit of Frobisher's sites. It was Walter Kenyon who first interested Jim Tuck and myself — both archaeologists at Memorial University of Newfoundland at the time — in the island that we would finally see fifteen years later.

The most recent phase of archaeological interest in Kodlunarn Island began at the Smithsonian Institution, with the rediscovery of the "proof" that Hall had collected, which had subsequently been misplaced along with the other Frobisher relics. It was found in a remote part of the Smithsonian's history collections by historian Wilcomb Washburn, who recognized it as an iron bloom. This round, pocked, and rusted object weighing about ten kilograms was the product of the type of small smelting furnace that was used throughout Europe in medieval times, but had been replaced by larger industrial furnaces in Elizabethan England. Intrigued by the discovery of such an incongruous object on Baffin Island, Washburn arranged to have radiocarbon tests run on the carbon contained in the iron, and in 1980 two measurements were obtained suggesting a date of the thirteenth or fourteenth century AD for the bloom. Such a date was consistent with the small size of the bloom and supported the suggestion of a pre-Frobisher age for the object. It was proposed that this iron bloom might not have been brought to the island by Frobisher, but that it might relate to an earlier occupation and be evidence of a previously unsuspected occupation of Baffin Island by the Greenlandic Norse.

Stimulated by this possibility, a Smithsonian expedition under archaeologist William Fitzhugh landed on the island in 1981. Three more iron blooms were found by using metal detectors, and test excavations were undertaken at most of the archaeological features on the island, but no definitive signs of a Norse presence were recovered. However, the newly found blooms also produced early radiocarbon dates, as did samples of charcoal recovered from the excavations, so the lure of a possible Norse occupation remained. By 1990 a more extensive expedition was planned, as a Smithsonian contribution to the celebration of the five hundredth anniversary of Columbus's voyage to America. This project was to investigate the possible Norse presence in the area, as well as carry out extensive excavations in the remains left by Frobisher's activities, in order to learn about Elizabethan mining and smelting technology and document how the local Inuit had made use of the Frobisher remains.

At this point the Canadian authorities became concerned over the question of whether a unique archaeological location that had been officially designated a National Historical Site could best be used to mark an American celebration. Since the designation of Kodlunarn Island as a site of national historical significance in 1964, nothing had been done to research, protect, or preserve the remains of the Frobisher expeditions. This neglect was somewhat embarrassing to Canadian authorities, faced with an offer from a foreign institution to do archaeological research on the island but with little apparent interest in its preservation as a unique historical landscape. In order to retain some control over the situation, they organized the Meta Incognita Committee, comprising representatives of several federal, territorial, and non-governmental agencies. This committee was meant to advise on the granting of permits for archaeological work, coordinate the research and other interests relating to the Frobisher sites, and stimulate archival and other historical research that would supplement the information which could be gained by archaeology.

The Meta Incognita Committee provided me with my first opportunity to visit Kodlunarn Island. Three of us — Charles Arnold, of the Prince of Wales Northern Heritage Centre in Yellowknife, Jim Tuck, and myself — arrived at the island on a summer day in 1990, charged with assessing the remains of sixteenth-century English activities and the dangers that threatened these archaeological remains. We were joined there by Bill Fitzhugh and Réginald Auger of the Smithsonian Institution, who were interested in excavating the structures and caches left by the English. Tuck and I returned the following summer for a longer period and with a larger crew, to complete the assessment and recommend a course for preserving the historical landscape in the face of natural erosion, increasing tourist interest, and the archaeological research projects planned by Fitzhugh and Auger. Those of us on these expeditions were fortunate that Tuck, an old and valued friend and colleague whose excavations of Basque whaling stations in southern Labrador had made him the leading expert on sixteenth-century European industrial enterprises in northern North America, could be involved. It was he who usually explained to the rest of us the possible interpretation of vague arrangements of boulders, and who usually identified the bits of broken pottery and other materials that littered the surface.

When we arrived in 1990, Kodlunarn Island looked much as it must have appeared shortly after Frobisher left, and after the Inuit had demolished the standing buildings in search of wood and iron nails. Walter Kenyon had remarked, "It still seems strange to me that Hall could find traces of Frobisher's smaller camps still visible after the passage of 300 years, and that I could find them just as easily after another 100 years." Fifteen years later these traces still lay relatively untouched.

A tour of the island can be completed on foot in half an hour. It is best to start at the rocky midpoint of the northern shore. This is one of the few places at which the surface of the island can be reached without scaling vertical sea cliffs. The visitor ascends along the steeply sloping floor of a narrow notch cut through the rock by Frobisher's miners. Hall named this feature the "Ship's Trench," since Inuit legend stated that the ancient *qadlunaat* had used it as a slipway to build a ship. This was probably the first mine opened in 1577, and the marks of hand mining are still clearly apparent along a vertical rock face forming one side of the mine. Kenyon noted, "All of Frobisher's vertical cuts were fresh and clear, and looked as though they might have been made last week." Mounds of spoil are heaped at either side of the mine, and a small pile of black ore lies where it was discarded.

The scars made by mining tools are still clearly visible on the walls of the mine at the northern end of the Countess of Warwick's Island (Canadian Museum of Civilization; photo Robert McGhee).

A field of packed boulders slopes gently upward from the top of the trench to the summit of the island. To the left of the trench lies a relatively flat area a little more than a hectare in extent, with a surface of silt and gravel. This was apparently a centre of English activity, and the remains of that activity are still very apparent. A few oval-to-rectangular patterns of boulders probably mark the locations of Elizabethan tents, while two scattered heaps of stones may once have covered small caches of supplies. An oblong boulder standing in a level, silty patch of ground may possibly be a crude headstone marking the burial of an English miner or seaman.

The most prominent human-made feature lies at the southwestern edge of this area. It is a large trench 25 metres long and 5 metres wide, which Hall called the "Reservoir or Mine." Inuit told him that they used this trench as a water source, and although it holds water during the early summer, it is very unlikely to have ever served as a reservoir. It is definitely a mine, and the orientation is the same as that of the Ship's Trench, as if a single vein of ore was being followed across the island. As in the Ship's Trench, earth and rock spoil are heaped on the surface to either side, and there is a pile of discarded ore at the southwestern end.

From the Reservoir, a shallow grass-covered valley about a quarter-hectare in extent slopes eastward to the coast. Four jumbled piles of boulders and turf emerge from the surface vegetation, apparently the remains of foundations for at least two small crude structures about five metres across, as well as less defined features. These structures were probably Frobisher's assay shops, where preliminary tests were run on the ores brought back from various mines in the vicinity. Tiny pieces of coal, charcoal, and smelting slag and fragments of small assay crucibles bear witness to late-medieval industrial activities.

The feature that has attracted the greatest archaeological attention in the past lies among rock outcrops at the highest point of the island. This is the small house or watchtower built at the end of the final Frobisher expedition and appointed with objects selected to entice Inuit interest. What remains today is a jumble of boulders lying amid a pile of mortar and plaster fragments. The foundations appear to have been thoroughly dug over, and all the artifacts left by the Frobisher party have long since been removed. Yet this small tumbled ruin, lying in isolation at the summit of Kodlunarn Island, should be appreciated as a remarkable heritage object, since it is the remains of the first recorded house built by the English in the New World.

Over a period of two weeks in the late summer of 1991 we completed a number of projects on Kodlunarn Island. Lee Jablonski, an engineer who donated his time and expertise, completed the first accurate map of the island and its archaeological remains. Donald Hogarth, a geologist from the University of Ottawa who had for some time worked on the Frobisher mines and the ore they produced, assessed the geological evidence for natural erosion on the island. Rob MacIntosh, a student

Engraving of crucibles and other refractory ceramics (from Agricola's *De re metallica*; photo Harry Foster)

from Arctic College in Iqaluit, made a comprehensive plant collection from the vegetated industrial portion of the site, information that would be useful in estimating the amount of damage which this small meadow could sustain from the trampling feet of tourists and the rate at which it might recover from such damage.

One of our first efforts involved a cairn that stood beside the Fenton watchtower at the island's summit. This cairn had been built from boulders taken from the fallen walls of the watchtower, crudely cemented with badly mixed and crumbling mortar. The hollow interior of the cairn contained a weathered Inuit skull. On the side of the structure was wired a brass plaque proclaiming the following message:

> THIS CAIRN WAS ERECTED
> IN MEMORY OF
> **SIR MARTIN FROBISHER**
> AS A CENTENNIAL PROJECT BY
> **LT. A. BROCKLEY**
> **DR. R. WEST**
> **MR. V. BROCKLEY**
> FROBISHER BAY 11.7.66

A rash of privately erected plaques and cairns marking personal visits to the Arctic have recently begun to appear at remote historic locations in Arctic Canada. In attempting to decide what should be done with this unsightly structure, we noted that the names of the three perpetrators were given the same size and prominence as that of Martin Frobisher. We therefore drew the conclusion that the cairn was really meant to commemorate these twentieth-century citizens and that an association with the Frobisher site was not warranted. I took responsibility for demolishing the cairn, and Jim Tuck and I removed the boulders to their original location; reburied the skull in an empty Inuit grave on the island, from which it had probably been removed; cleaned up the crumbled mortar and disposed of it in the sea; and presented the plaque to the Prince of Wales Northern Heritage Centre, the official museum of the Northwest Territories.

Most of our archaeological efforts were devoted to three areas of interest: the Ship's Trench, the Fenton watchtower at the summit of the island, and the workshop structures in the industrial area. The Ship's Trench was seen as the most likely place where we might find buried and cached material left by the English. One account of the final Frobisher voyage states that, before leaving the island, "We buried the timber of our pretended fort, with many barrels of meal, peas, grist and sundry other good things." Another account reports that these things were "hidden and covered in the place of the mine." The search for this cached material was begun

Archaeological excavations in the Ship's Trench mine during the summer of 1991 recovered the remains of buried supplies (Canadian Museum of Civilization; photo Robert McGhee).

by digging a trench across the mine at a location just above the level of high storm tides. As this is the deepest portion of the trench, it would be the place where frozen and preserved material would most likely be found, and it would be the location that would provide evidence of the shipbuilding reported for this locale by Inuit legend. Importantly, the heavy boulders covering the surface in this area would allow us to easily disguise the scars of our excavation.

After removing these boulders, the excavators began scraping and sifting through a jumble of broken rock and silty soil, occasionally finding small fragments of red ceramic tile, charcoal, and preserved wood and one small, unidentifiable piece of rusted iron. Most of the wood fragments appeared to be of oak and were quite possibly the remains of broken barrel staves; this conjecture was supported by the finding of several lengths of split willow or osier, identical to the sixteenth-century barrel hoops found at Basque sites in Labrador. We also found evidence of what some of these barrels had contained; numerous small round black objects could be easily identified as dried peas that had been carbonized in the soil. We also found many amorphous lumps of a black organic material, which was more difficult to identify, but which we guessed to be the carbonized remains of ship's biscuit. This staple food of northern maritime enterprise is still used in Newfoundland, and we had some Newfoundland hard bread in our own supplies. We were thus able to conduct a small experiment by carbonizing some hard-bread on our camp stove, where it turned into a substance which was visually identical to that which we found in the trench. The Canadian Conservation Institute in Ottawa later undertook an analysis and inconclusive identification of the material which suggests that this very unappetizing substance may well be four-hundred-year-old ship's biscuit.

The material filling the base of the old mine extended to a depth of at least 1.5 metres, by which point we judged our excavation to be close to bedrock and too sus-

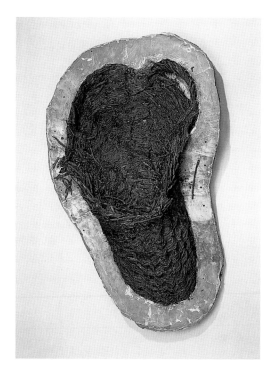

Portion of a basket preserved by permafrost in the Ship's Trench mine at the north end of Kodlunarn Island (Canadian Museum of Civilization; photo Steven Darby)

ceptible to collapse for safe work. By the time we had abandoned and refilled our trench, however, it had told us what we wanted to discover. We had found the place where the Frobisher expedition had buried the supplies for its planned colony, "hidden and covered in the place of the mine," as reported by Edward Sellman. The men had probably covered the cache with a thick layer of boulders, but this cannot have prevented the Inuit from soon learning of this deposit. A major salvage operation must have begun within a few days or weeks of Frobisher's departure, in order to recover such valued materials as hardwoods and iron nails. The deposit appears to have been thoroughly quarried, and only the discarded remnants that were left behind are now available to archaeology.

The Inuit traditions that Hall recorded, which are still related around Frobisher Bay, tell that a ship was built in this rocky trench by the five marooned *qadlunaat* for which Kodlunarn Island is named, and that its two masts had been set into place at a location called Nepouetiesupbing on the adjacent mainland shore. It was on the basis of these traditions that Hall named the mine the "Ship's Trench," and while excavating this trench, we were watching for evidence of shipbuilding activities. However, neither our excavations nor those carried out in subsequent years by Réginald Auger provided significant evidence that a ship had been built here.

To what, then, does the Inuit tradition refer? If the five marooned *qadlunaat* who are reported to have built a ship on Kodlunarn Island are considered to be the same as the five sailors lost by Frobisher in 1576 at a location over a hundred kilometres to the west, it seems highly unlikely that these men would have remained hidden from the English for two years and then have travelled to Kodlunarn Island after the English had gone. It has been suggested that they may have been a different group of sailors lost during the panic of September 1578, or that the story relates to a later period when the marooning of whaling crews and instances of crews jumping ship and attempting to escape by boat were not unheard of on the Arctic whaling grounds.

Furthermore, the steeply sloping Ship's Trench on Kodlunarn Island seems a very unlikely place in which to build a ship, especially since we now know that the sea level there during the sixteenth century was not much different from today's. Such a chore could be much more easily accomplished on many of the low and protected shores that exist within a few kilometres of the island. Given the nature of the terrain and the absence of archaeological evidence, it seems likely that the tradition is an amalgam of several elements that have been collapsed over four centuries of oral transmission. These elements might include the five sailors lost by Frobisher in 1576 on the southwestern shore of Frobisher Bay, the English mining activities on Kodlunarn Island in 1577 and 1578, the beaching and repair of the badly leaking *Anne Frances* somewhere near Kodlunarn Island in late August 1578, and the large cache of wood and provisions salvaged by the Inuit from the Ship's Trench. By the time of Hall's visit in the 1860s, all the useful material had been removed from the cache, but Inuit continued to visit the island in order to collect fragments of red clay roofing tiles, which were powdered and used to burnish the brass headbands that were worn by the women of the period. The archaeological evidence of the past English presence would have made Kodlunarn Island a magnet for any traditions associated with *qadlunaat* in Frobisher Bay, and the collapsing of such traditions into a single comprehensible story that occurred at a specific place is characteristic of oral history everywhere in the world.

Having satisfied ourselves that the Ship's Trench held nothing but the scattered remains of the main cache left behind by the English, we turned our attention to the house that the Frobisher expedition had built at the top of the island. Here we were careful in selecting areas where minimal excavation would tell us how much of the original structure was left. We soon found, to our surprise, that much of the foundation was intact, despite the disturbance that had tumbled the walls and churned up the interior of the building. The walls were built of boulders that had been roughly hewn into shape and cemented with lime mortar; the yellowish mortar fragments that litter the area contain small nodules of English flint, indicating that the mortar had been brought aboard ship.

The single room of the house measures (in the English units that were used in designing it) 8 feet by 10 feet on the inside; each wall is 2 feet thick, and up to three courses of stone are still standing in places. The doorway probably lay under a pile of boulders at the southwestern corner of the room, a common location for the doorway and the adjacent hearth in English cottages of the time, but we left this corner

The remains of the house built by the English is still clearly visible on the summit of Kodlunarn Island. (Canadian Museum of Civilization; photo Robert McGhee).

Reproduction of the stone house built by Captain Edward Fenton on the summit of Kodlunarn Island in August 1578 (Canadian Museum of Civilization; photo Steven Darby)

undisturbed. We counted and measured about four hundred boulders that had fallen from the structure, giving us a very rough indication that the stone walls must have originally stood about one metre high. The roof was of wooden boards, which must have been among the first items on the island to be salvaged by the Inuit.

Our final project involved a search for other buried deposits or structures that might exist on the island. Since we wished to cause as little disturbance as possible, we enlisted the aid of Jean Pilon, a geophysicist with the Geological Survey of Canada. Pilon has worked in the development of ground-penetrating radar, which detects buried features by sending electromagnetic signals into the earth, and Kod-

Jean Pilon and assistants test the lower end of the Ship's Trench mine using ground-penetrating radar (Canadian Museum of Civilization; photo Robert McGhee).

lunarn Island tested the archaeological potential of this new technology. For three days we walked the radar instrument, which resembles a large pair of feet attached to handle frames, across the various features of the site. At every 10-centimetre step the machine beeped and sent a picture of the earth beneath it to a portable computer, where a profile view of the subterranean feature gradually built up across the screen. Our first set of traverses covered the area around the possible headstone, and the radar received signals suggesting that, indeed, there was something buried about one metre deep to one side of the stone. The machine could not tell whether this object was a human body or a large isolated boulder, but since the signal came from what appears to be an area of uniform gravelly soil, the possibility of a human interment seems quite high.

We also made radar transects across the remains of the assaying and metallurgical workshops in the industrial portion of the site. These showed that there were no stone floors, buried furnaces, or other major buried features of the structures, and that little would be learned by excavation. We were particularly happy with this result, since excavation of these structures would have scarred the only vegetated area on the island. In fact, two barren patches of earth near the structures almost certainly mark areas where the surface vegetation was dug up four hundred years ago, to provide insulation for the walls of Frobisher's workshops.

Neither in our work on the island nor in that done in subsequent years under the Meta Incognita Committee was any trace found of a Norse or any other European presence. The iron blooms that had originally stimulated the idea that Kodlunarn Island might have seen a medieval occupation were almost certainly brought to the area by Frobisher's crews. Historians have pointed out an unusual item in Michael Lok's meticulous accounts relating to outfitting the 1577 voyage: "paid for v^c, of yron stones of Russia at iiij^d pece li beinge vj tons for balliste for the *Gabriel*." Translated from the roman numerical system, this item states that five hundred iron stones from Russia were bought at 4 pence apiece to make up six tons of ballast for the *Gabriel*. The average weight of an "iron stone of Russia" would therefore be twenty-four pounds (approximately eleven kilograms), which compares reasonably well with the average weight of approximately twenty pounds (nine kilograms) for

Artifacts recovered from Kodlunarn Island: (at the top) two fragments of glazed tile from a German stove, one bearing the date 1561 and the other the head of a mythological figure; (centre left) a fragment of an assaying crucible containing slag; (bottom left) a fragment of a ceramic muffle used in the assaying furnace; (bottom right) a ceramic roof tile (courtesy Réginald Auger; photo Steven Darby)

the four blooms collected from Kodlunarn Island. There seems little doubt that the blooms were the obsolete product of a Russian smelting industry, which were recycled as an efficient and easily handled ballast. They may have been well travelled before being imported by the Muscovy Company as ballast on their ships and transferred to the *Gabriel* in the Thames. When the ballast was discharged in the Countess of Warwick Sound, a number of blooms may have been brought ashore, where they could have proved useful for a number of purposes, including an emergency source of iron. Eventually they became curiosities to the Inuit of Baffin Island, who seem to have distributed them widely around the countryside adjacent to Frobisher's mines.

During our stay on Kodlunarn Island, we had managed to learn what we wished without inflicting much visible damage on the landscape. We located the supplies that had been cached for the eventual establishment of a colony and had found that they had long since been salvaged by the Inuit. We learned that the house or watchtower at the top of the island would repay a small and careful excavation, and we buried it until such a dig could be undertaken. We proved that none of the other structures on the site had significant buried features. Most importantly, our survey had established the importance of preservation as a basic principle of archaeological work at a site of such unique value. The excavation that was carried out by Réginald Auger in subsequent years, which recovered additional information from the Ship's Trench and other locations, has respected this principle.

When one walks over Kodlunarn Island on a summer day, no obvious signs of modern activity intrude on the sense of history. This is still Frobisher's Countess of Warwick's Island, the site of the first Canadian gold rush and the first attempt to plant an English settlement in the Americas, where the remains of Elizabethan activities are still a clearly visible part of the scene. The sense of a historic landscape, a place where one is in touch with the past, is very fragile, and we must hope that it can be maintained at this special site.

Fifteen

A FINAL ASSAY

MORE THAN FOUR CENTURIES HAVE NOW ELAPSED since Martin Frobisher ventured to Arctic Canada, surely enough time to allow an accurate assessment of his accomplishments, as well as of the unintended results of this episode in the history of northern North America. The historical judgment on his accomplishments is inevitably coloured by the major failures that were so clearly and savagely identified in Michael Lok's "The Abuses of Captayn Furbusher Agaynst the Companye." In sum, Frobisher failed in his undertaking to find a Northwest Passage to Asia, he failed in his commission to establish an English settlement in Meta Incognita, and his mining venture in Arctic Canada resulted only in losses to the reputations and finances of all those involved.

From today's perspective, it is clear that two of these failures were inevitable. Frobisher may be derided for mistaking the enclosed Frobisher Bay for a strait to Asia, but we now know that such a strait did not exist. The northwestern route from Atlantic to Pacific is a long and tortuous series of ice-choked channels that could not be traversed with the aid of maritime technologies less advanced than those of the twentieth century. Similarly, the failure to establish the planned hundred-man colony in Meta Incognita should be recognized as an example of Frobisher's good judgment, since an attempt to winter in the area would have been disastrous to men dependent on sixteenth-century shelter, clothing, and provisions.

The third failure – that of the mining enterprise – cannot be so easily dismissed, and it remains a mystery that has yet to be adequately explained. Several historians and geologists have recently attempted to illuminate this dark corner of the Frobisher venture and have devised a variety of excuses and accusations relating to those

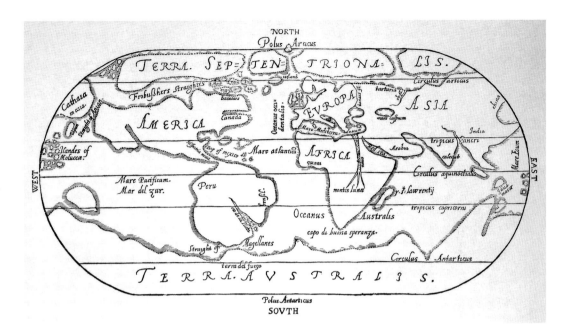

Map of the world drawn by James Beare, principal surveyor of the expedition, showing Frobisher's newly discovered lands (from Stefansson and McCaskill 1938; photo Harry Foster)

involved in the promoting, prospecting, and assaying sides of the project. With these studies in hand, and now that four centuries have passed since the deaths of the principal characters, we can attempt an independent audit of the enterprise.

The most intensive investigation has been undertaken by geologist Donald Hogarth. To begin, he used modern assaying methods to test sixty-six samples of rock that should represent most of the ores mined by Frobisher's men; fifty-four of these were collected from various mine sites in Frobisher Bay, seven from the vicinity of the Manor House at Dartford where the ore was stored for smelting, and five from the remains of the *Emmanuel*'s cargo at Smerwick in Ireland. None of the samples contained pyrites, the "fool's gold" that is often assumed to have misled Frobisher and his prospectors. All were "black ore," igneous and metamorphic rocks rich in the dark mineral hornblende, combined with feldspars and other minerals. Half the samples contained less gold than the average in the earth's crust, while the others had about the average proportion for rocks of this type. None had any appreciable quantity of precious metal, and the amounts of gold and silver were

so small that they could not have been detected by sixteenth-century assaying techniques. Twentieth-century mineral prospecting has not produced evidence of significant gold deposits in any location around Frobisher Bay, so it is very improbable that any of the ores mined by Frobisher's crews were significantly richer than Hogarth's samples. The amount of gold reported in some of the sixteenth-century assays would indicate a gold content from two hundred times to over forty thousand times that found in Hogarth's rock samples. There is therefore no question that the assays on various "black ores" produced incorrect results, and the only problem lies in discovering the causes of these results.

Historian Robert Baldwin has suggested that the initial findings of gold may have been conditioned by the expectation that the New World was rich in deposits of precious metals. The Spanish had found silver throughout the conquered districts of Mexico, Peru was seemingly awash in gold, and only a generation earlier Jacques Cartier had reported diamonds and precious metals from the "River of Canada." John Dee expected to find gold deposits along the northern passage to Cathay equivalent to those that the Spanish had developed in the Moluccas along the southern route. More specifically, prospectors of the period were familiar with the metallurgist Vannuccio Biringuccio's theory that rocky and watery landforms generated gold, raising expectations that the metal would be found in barren coastal localities such as those that Frobisher had discovered. Other, more bizarre theories of the time also came into play: in his account of the 1577 voyage, Dionyse Settle noted the presence in Meta Incognita of spiders "which as many affirme, are signes of great store of gold." Aside from their preconceptions, Frobisher's crews encountered rocks that actually looked as if they were valuable. After his 1974 visit to the Countess of Warwick Sound, archaeologist Walter Kenyon wrote, "And I could see why Frobisher and his men believed that the country was incredibly rich in minerals. For many of the rock outcrops sparkled on a sunny day like jewels, with the glitter of feldspar, quartz, quartzite and mica."

Such expectations may have led to the initial assumption that the rock which Frobisher brought from the Arctic in 1576 should be tested for precious metals. However, in themselves they do not explain the results of these tests. Historian

Map of the Arctic regions published in 1606 by the Flemish cartographer Gerhard Mercator, incorporating Frobisher's discoveries (Royal Ontario Museum)

Bernard Allaire has pointed out the inadequacy of sixteenth-century chemical knowledge in providing a basis for the accurate assessment of the metal content of ores. Ingredients were impure and measuring instruments relatively inaccurate, but more important was the lack of understanding about chemical processes. The practising chemists and assayers of the period distinguished themselves from medieval alchemists on the basis of what they had learned from practical experience, rather than from a difference in underlying theories about how materials formed and interacted. Allaire also indicates that sixteenth-century legal documents contain numerous references to fraud by assayers and refiners of precious metals, and he notes several techniques that were known to have been practised. Among the simpler and more ingenious techniques were double-bottomed crucibles, in which powdered gold or silver was hidden beneath a false bottom that dissolved during the smelting process. A similar result could be obtained by packing powdered metal into a hollow wooden rod, which burned and released its contents when it was used to stir the molten ore.

The technical aspect that several authors suggest as a means by which either error or deliberate fraud could have occurred was the silver and gold present in the materials which were added to the ore during the smelting process. This contamination could originate either in the lead or zinc ores that were used as a flux in order to assist in the melting of the rock or in the lead that was added near the end of the process to amalgamate with the precious metal and separate it from the slag. In either case, at the end of the assay it was impossible to tell whether the resulting gold and silver had come from the ore or from the additives. The presence of precious metals in these substances was known to metallurgists of the time, and it was general practice, then as later, to subtract an estimate of this material from the result in order to obtain a true assay. Ignoring the contamination from additives provided a simple means of obtaining a rich assay, but such a procedure must have been deliberate fraud and not unsuspected error. In addition, many of the Frobisher assays were so rich that, if the contamination did originate in the additives, it would have been immediately apparent that the additives provided a valuable ore which was available much closer and less expensively than rock from Baffin Island.

It seems clear that fraud was practised at several points in the venture and probably by several unconnected parties. It must have begun with Giovanni Battista Agnello, the only assayer whose results indicated a high value for the original rock brought back by Frobisher in 1576. Agnello was an alchemist rather than an assayer or refiner, and he admitted to Michael Lok that he had had no experience with precious metals. His obscure explanation for his successful assay — "One must know how to flatter nature" — may have referred to the simple sleight of hand which would have been all that was needed to present Lok with the gold powder that he claimed to have recovered from the unpromising black rock. As for motive, all that may have been required was the desire of a foreign resident in an insecure position to advance his status and acquaintance with the merchants and courtiers of London. Lok and Frobisher may be accused of credulity, and in fact, they must have welcomed the assay as a means of providing support for a second venture to Baffin Island, but there is no indication that they were involved in provoking or developing the fraud.

Jonas Schutz, who served as assayer on the 1577 expedition, is somewhat more difficult to understand. He was a German immigrant who had developed a considerable reputation in England as a mining engineer. He had worked with Agnello and may have learned from him the techniques of "flattering nature," although his motives for undertaking such a practice are obscure. In fact, Schutz's assaying work during the 1577 voyage is not well documented, and it appears that he rejected the "black ore" of the Countess of Warwick's Island in favour of "red ore" from the locality known as Jonas' Mount. Geologist Donald Hogarth suggests, on the basis of little evidence, that in fact Schutz may have located a red sandy "gossan" deposit that contained a significant amount of gold but was never again rediscovered. Although Schutz's work during the 1577 voyage may have been blameless, by the following winter he was obviously involved in fraudulent assays. At this time he and Burchard Kranich were engaged in a competition to contract for the major smelting operation planned at Dartford, and the optimistic assays produced by both parties seem to have been aimed at gaining the contract. Kranich was the oddest of an odd lot of assayers, and no one seems to have been surprised when he was caught out in the deliberate fraud of February 1578. By then, however, the momentum of the venture seems to have been so great that the small and understandable deception of an ill and greedy old man could not stand in its way.

The assayer whose results are most difficult to interpret is Robert Denham, the experienced refiner who acted as the commission's spy in discovering Kranich's duplicity and went on to serve as assayer for the 1578 voyage. From his assay shop on the Countess of Warwick's Island, he evaluated ores from all the deposits mined. The results of these assays were lost when the sea washed through Frobisher's cabin on the *Aid*, but some or even most of them must have been optimistic in view of the amount of black rock that was collected on that expedition.

As noted in an earlier chapter, Denham was the only assayer whose reputation and career survived his involvement in the Frobisher venture. His apparent competence and trustworthiness are at odds with the assay results that he produced during the 1578 expedition, and it is difficult to detect the motive that would have led him to produce such results. The fact that faulty assays were being made on the Countess of Warwick's Island by an apparently trusted employee bears a very specific resemblance to a much more recent and better documented gold-mining fraud: the Bre-X affair. Other similarities are easily seen between the Frobisher and Bre-X ventures: each involved gold deposits in a remote and poorly known region, and deposits that were far richer and more extensive than those found in more familiar countries; both developed over a similar period of time; and each was incredibly successful in involving large numbers of seasoned investors in a scheme which, in hindsight, had very little credibility. A brief look at Bre-X may bring us closer to understanding the Frobisher story.

In 1989 a little-known Canadian mining promoter named David Walsh formed a penny-stock company called Bre-X Minerals, as a means of raising capital for mining exploration. He issued one million shares at 30 cents per share, and for the following three years the company promoted several worthless gold and diamond properties in northern Canada and Arizona. By 1993 Bre-X Minerals had few remaining assets, and Walsh himself had been declared bankrupt. At this time he happened to contact a geologist named John Felderhof, who persuaded him to use his last resources to buy an interest in a gold property named Busang in the Kalimantan district of the island of Borneo in Indonesian. Felderhof was a widely experienced Canadian geologist who had been involved in several major discoveries but had never struck it rich himself. The Australian mining company for which he worked had explored the Busang property extensively and had not found enough gold to encourage development, but Felderhof thought that it still had value.

In May 1993 Walsh announced to the public that Bre-X had invested in a property which had the potential to produce a million ounces of gold, and he set about raising money to explore Busang with an extensive drilling program. In a very innovative move for the time, he opened an Internet site on the newly established World Wide Web and encouraged the use of Internet chat rooms and discussion forums for disseminating information, rumours, gossip, and opinion regarding Bre-X's potential. By the end of 1993 the value of Bre-X stock had more than doubled to almost 30 cents per share, the price at which it had originally been listed four years earlier.

Felderhof became Bre-X's chief geologist and general manager. If Walsh the promoter was to play the role of a minor-league Michael Lok, then Felderhof's role would have been that of Jonas Schutz, although his mining credentials included considerably greater experience and reputation. As word of the potentially massive gold find in Indonesia spread, it attracted the attention of several reputable and experienced investors and mining developers – the Winters, the Dudleys, and perhaps the Frobishers of the twentieth-century venture. For the role of Robert Denham, Felderhof hired an old associate, a Filipino geologist named Michael de Guzman, who was placed in charge of the work at Busang, supervising drilling operations, logging drill cores, and sending assay samples to laboratories. De Guzman staffed his crew with other Filipino geologists, who were paid considerably less than those from Australia or North America.

The following three years saw an increasing number of drill holes sunk into the massive 350-square-kilometre Busang deposit, an accelerating amount of optimistic information and even more optimistic rumour concerning the results of the drilling, and a concurrent increase in the value of Bre-X stock. By May 1995 the shares were worth over $4 Canadian, an increase of more than 1,000 per cent from their original price. By July 1995 the estimated gold reserves had increased to more than two million ounces and the price of shares had doubled again. Two days later the estimate was raised to eight million ounces and in August to thirteen million. In November an estimate of thirty million ounces produced a stock price above $50. Large volumes of new shares were issued to satisfy the demand from small investors throughout Canada and elsewhere, especially after the stock listing moved from the tiny Calgary exchange to those in Toronto and New York. By the spring of 1996 over a million shares a day were being traded at prices higher than $250. Those who had invested as little as $1,000 two years earlier were now millionaires. In early 1997 the estimate of gold from the Busang property had surpassed fifty million ounces, and major mining companies were competing to get in on the action. The bidding finally went to an American giant, Freeport, which planned its own drilling program before finalizing the deal to develop a mine at the site.

The Bre-X story culminated on March 9, 1997, a day when Felderhof, Walsh, and de Guzman were the toast of the annual meeting of the Prospectors and Developers Association of Canada, and Felderhof was presented with an award as "Explorationist of the Year." Ten days later Michael de Guzman fell or jumped from a helicopter taking him to Busang to meet the Freeport geologists, who had been unable to find any trace of gold in their first drill cores. This discrepancy came on top of rumours from the assay labs that the gold from Bre-X's Busang cores was not in the form of angular particles, as would be expected, but in rounded grains such as that panned from river deposits. The value of Bre-X stock collapsed. Walsh and Felderhof moved to Caribbean tax havens, while vigorously defending their estimates of the Busang deposit's value. The ensuing investigations and commercial suits never clarified the details of the Bre-X fraud, nor did they succeed in apportioning blame to the satisfaction of investors, but the broad outlines of a very simple scheme became apparent.

The groundwork had most likely been carried out by de Guzman himself or with the help of his underpaid assistants, and was done by the time-honoured technique of "salting" assay samples. Alluvial gold purchased from local Dayak miners had been introduced into sample bags of crushed rock, according to a pattern that could have been known and understood only by the geologist supervising the drilling and logging of cores. As in the case of Robert Denham on the Countess of Warwick's Island, the motive for the undertaking is not entirely clear. De Guzman stood to profit through the sale of inflated Bre-X shares, but he owned only a small fraction of the stock held by other members of the company, and he made no effort to sell stock or advise his friends and family to do so as the final and inevitable collapse approached. As in the case of Jonas Schutz and Burchard Kranich during the winter of 1577–78, the motive may have simply been an effort to continue employment in a position that would ultimately be proved profitable. De Guzman, probably like his Elizabethan predecessors, seems to have worked from the assumption that the property did contain gold, but that deception was required to maintain the search until a way was found to discover or smelt the metal actually hidden in the rocks.

No convincing evidence was recovered to link the major figures in Bre-X Minerals to the fraud. Felderhof, a competent geologist with knowledge of local conditions, must have at least suspected the increasingly optimistic assays, but he may have been blinded to the truth by his belief in the profitability of the deposit and the knowledge that after a long career he had finally struck it extremely rich. To promoter David Walsh the geology of Busang may have been a mystery that was simply not relevant to his interests in raising money and selling shares. Although he can be accused of manipulating information and share prices, he may well have believed that the underlying value of Busang was worth everything he told his stockholders.

In sum, the extreme success of the Bre-X venture may have lain in the very low level at which the fraudulent activity occurred and the separation of this activity from the upper levels of the organization. Could John Felderhof have given as convincing performances in presenting his absurd estimates of up to two hundred million ounces of gold if he was certain that the estimates were based on fraud? Could David Walsh have sold Busang as plausibly if he had known that it was of no more value than any of the other phony mineral deposits he had tried and failed to promote throughout his career?

The Bre-X analogy encourages us to examine the players in the Frobisher gold-mining venture in a new light. At a time when the salting of assay samples was much more easily accomplished than during the 1990s, such a procedure was open to anyone such as Agnello, Schutz, Kranich, or Denham who had a very rudimentary knowledge of assaying. None of these individuals stood to gain immense personal profits from his activities, but perhaps we should look for motive at a much lower level: continuance of employment, preferment in a contract, or acquaintance with wealthy and powerful merchants and courtiers. As may have been the case at Busang, the astonishing success of the Frobisher fraud may have been related to the implicit belief of the promoters and organizers of the venture that there was immense value in the rocks. In their most heated litigations Martin Frobisher and Michael Lok accused each other of every form of mismanagement but not of involvement in a deliberate fraud. Certainly, there is nothing in the behaviour of Lok, Frobisher, Sir William Winter, or others involved at a high level to indicate anything but the suspicion that these men were blinded by visions of extreme personal wealth. As the Canadian public demonstrated during the 1990s, human nature has changed little over four centuries.

(A disclaimer: I hold a small investment in Bre-X Minerals. Having been involved in the Frobisher story throughout the 1990s and developed an interest in mining scams, I could not help but be fascinated by the Bre-X venture. I resisted personal involvement until a few days after Michael de Guzman's helicopter accident, when share prices had dropped by over 90 per cent and the world knew that a fraud was in progress. Speculation at the time was divided between those who thought that the fraud had been perpetrated by Bre-X and those who suggested that vast fortunes were to be made in destroying its credibility. My shares now have only curiosity value, but the financial loss was compensated for by the experience I gained by participating in Canada's long and proud history of mining fraud.)

Despite the failure of the Frobisher venture in the fields of exploration, colonization, and mining, the project had one major and largely unintended historical consequence: the establishment of English sovereignty over northern North America. Although Frobisher collected "tokens of possession" and raised a cairn on Mount Warwick to proclaim Queen Elizabeth's ownership of Meta Incognita, neither of these acts had much consequence in themselves. More significant was John Dee's involvement in the venture and his concomitant interest in the establishment of what would become the British Empire. While instructing Frobisher and his officers in navigation during the spring of 1576, Dee was writing a manual titled *General and Rare Memorials Pertayning to the Perfect Art of Navigation*. He hoped that by increasing the navigational skills of English seamen, he would lay the foundations for British sovereignty overseas, and the first volume was accordingly entitled *The British Monarchy*, or *Hexameron Brytannicum*.

In 1578, at the conclusion of the Frobisher voyages, Queen Elizabeth asked Dee to produce an argument for her claim to the northern lands that he had described. It is unclear whether he accomplished this task immediately or whether the document that he presented to the Queen in October 1580 was the first result of his efforts. This document exists in the form of a large rolled parchment in the collections of the British Library. On one side is a map centred on North America, showing a wide northern sea containing Frobisher's discoveries in Meta Incognita as well as several mythical islands that originated on the Zeno map. On the reverse side of the parchment is a long and detailed statement laying out the basis for Queen Elizabeth's sovereignty over this northern world. The argument is derived almost entirely from historical precedent, beginning with the British king Arthur. Dee claims, on the basis of evidence that can at best be folklore and more probably came largely from his own mind, that Arthur "not only Conquered Iseland, Groenland, and all the Northern Iles cumpassing unto Russia, But even unto the North Pole (in manner) did extend his Jurisdiction: And sent Colonies thither, and into the Isles between Scotland and Iseland, whereby yt is probable that the late named Friseland Iseland is of the Brytish ancient Discovery and possession: And allso seeing Groeland beyond Groenland did receive their inhabitants by Arthur, yt is credible that the famous Iland Estotiland was by his folke possessed." Following in a mythological vein, he states as fact the legendary voyages to the New World by the Irish St Brendan around the year AD 560 and by the Welsh prince Owen Madoc around 1170. The supposed voyage in 1494 of Robert Thorn to Newfoundland and the similar voyage three years later that is attributed to Sebastian Cabot are also mentioned.

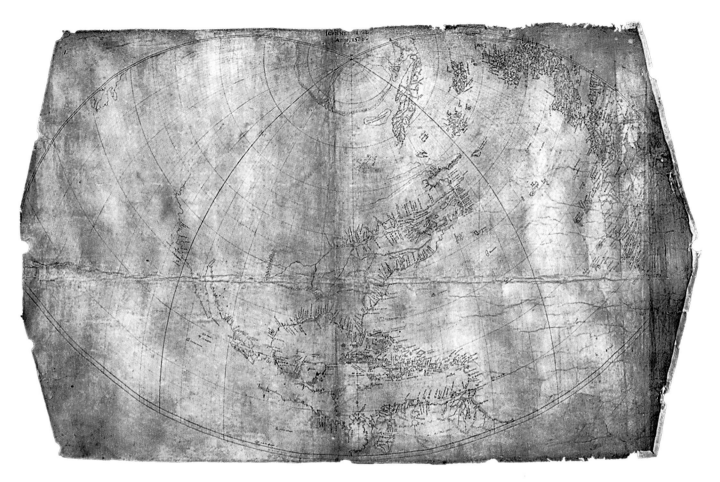

Coming to the current monarchy, Dee notes Martin Frobisher's claim of Meta Incognita for Queen Elizabeth. On the basis of these precedents, he argues "by force of Law" that the English monarch had a right to claim dominion over the northern portions of North America and the islands lying to the north of it.

John Dee was to put this claim into practice during the early 1580s, when he joined with Adrian Gilbert and John Davis to apply for a charter to explore, trade, and hold monopoly over these lands as "The colleagues of the fellowship of the New Navigations Atlantical and Septentrional." Under the exploration patent for

Map incorporating the Frobisher discoveries, drawn in 1580 by John Dee, who had provided Frobisher with navigational instruments and training (British Library)

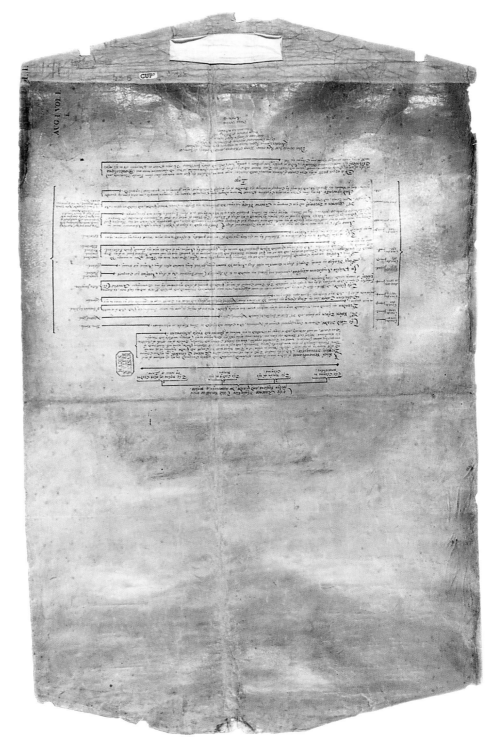

The reverse side of the John Dee map, containing a statement detailing English claims to sovereignty in the New World, based on Frobisher's Arctic discoveries as well as earlier mythological accounts relating to King Arthur, the Irish St Brendan, and the Welsh prince Owen Madoc (British Library)

eastern North America that was granted to Humphrey Gilbert, his brother Adrian gave Dee the rights to all New World lands to the north of 50° latitude, which would encompass most of what is now Canada. This grant may not have gone into effect, because it was in the same year of 1583 Dee suddenly left England to follow his mystical and alchemical pursuits in central Europe. However, by this time the plans to further Frobisher's exploration were being laid, and they were to culminate in the three expeditions led by John Davis to the eastern Canadian Arctic in 1585–87.

Davis, like Frobisher, had been instructed by Dee in navigation and geography, but he proved a much superior pupil. His three well-conducted expeditions returned with a great deal of geographical information regarding the western coast of Greenland and the eastern coasts of Baffin Island and Labrador. Most importantly for further exploration, he described and determined the correct latitude of the "very great gulfe" that lay off the northern tip of Labrador – Frobisher's Mistaken Straits, which is now known as Hudson Strait, the passage to the great inland sea at the heart of central Canada. The strait was again entered by the English sailor George Waymouth in 1602, and eight years later Henry Hudson explored the bay that now bears his name. By the early 1600s the Arctic channels of northern North America were recognized as an English sea. Within a century of Frobisher's voyages the English had established settlements at the lower end of Hudson Bay and were trading for furs and information far up the rivers of the Canadian prairies, bypassing the trading empire of the French in the St Lawrence and Mississippi valleys. The political, social, and linguistic character of northern North America is largely an unintended result of the explorations that began with Martin Frobisher.

Over the following centuries British exploration and commerce gradually penetrated Arctic Canada, and British claims to possession of the area were acceded to by most European nations. British sovereignty in the Arctic was passed to the new nation of Canada with the transfer of the northern mainland in 1870, followed by the islands of the Arctic archipelago in 1880. Throughout this time the principal occupants of the region were the Inuit, descendants of the people with whom Frobisher had traded and fought three centuries before. The Inuit remained secure in the knowledge that they had total sovereignty over the lands on which they lived,

The town of Iqaluit, capital of the new territory of Nunavut, lies at the head of Frobisher Bay only a few kilometres beyond the farthest point reached by the Frobisher ventures (photo Nick Newbery).

and they continued to welcome *qadlunaat*, with whom they carried out a profitable commerce. These *qadlunaat* came in the form of Scottish and American whalers in the late nineteenth century, fur traders in the early twentieth century, military personnel during and after World War II, and an increasing diversity of missionaries, police, teachers, and administrators. By the mid-twentieth century, Canadian law and the regulations of Canadian society had become so dominant that aboriginal sovereignty could no longer be assumed.

Most Inuit were disturbed by the idea that they had lost ownership of the lands that their ancestors had settled many generations before, and the latter half of the twentieth century saw an accelerating process of negotiation towards a settlement between aboriginal and governmental concepts of sovereignty. In 1993 the Tungavik Federation of Nunavut reached a land-claim agreement with Queen Elizabeth II in right of Canada which returns a measure of ownership and control to the descendants of the original Inuit occupants of the region. In 1999 the new territory of

Nunavut ("Our Land") was established, to be governed by an assembly elected by a population that is still predominantly Inuit. The capital of Nunavut is Iqaluit, a town at the head of Frobisher Bay in the very area where over four hundred years ago Martin Frobisher sought the Northwest Passage and claimed the land as a possession of Elizabeth I. The political changes that began as a result of his voyages have finally come full circle.

Sources and Selected Readings

This list covers the most widely accessible sources for important information about the Frobisher voyages. These books, together with the citations they contain, should refer readers to any further information that they may desire on subjects related to this venture.

Agricola, Georg. 1950 (1556). *De re metallica*. New York: Dover. An English translation of the classic mid-sixteenth-century treatise on mining and metallurgy, the work that was most likely to have been known by most of the prospectors, miners, and assayers associated with the Frobisher venture.

Alsford, Stephen, ed. 1993. *The Meta Incognita Project: Contributions to Field Studies*. Hull: Canadian Museum of Civilization. A series of brief reports summarizing archaeological work carried out on both English and Inuit sites in Frobisher Bay during 1990 and 1991, by various scholars associated with the Meta Incognita Project.

Collinson, Richard, ed. 1867. *The Three Voyages of Martin Frobisher in Search of a Passage to Cathaia and India by the North-West, 1576–78*. Hakluyt Society, series 1, no. 38. London. Rear-Admiral Richard Collinson, himself an Arctic naval explorer, compiled and reprinted what remains the most complete collection of original documents and accounts related to the Frobisher voyages.

Fitzhugh, William W., and Jacqueline S. Olin, eds. 1993. *Archaeology of the Frobisher Voyages*. Washington: Smithsonian Institution. The papers in this volume summarize the results of the Smithsonian's 1981, 1990, and 1991 archaeological work in Frobisher Bay, as well as analytical work on objects related to the Frobisher sites. Caution should be exercised in judging some of the interpretations presented, since these papers were written at a time when some authors considered Kodlunarn Island to show evidence of a Norse occupation.

French, Peter J. 1972. *John Dee: The World of an Elizabethan Magus*. London: Routledge and Kegan Paul. Many of the accessible works on John Dee are written from the mystical fringes of scholarship. In contrast, this excellent monograph provides a rounded assessment of the man and his contributions to history.

Hall, Charles Frances. 1865. *Life with the Esquimaux: A narrative of Arctic Experience in Search of Survivors of Sir John Franklin's Expedition*. London: Sampson, Low, Son, and Marston; repr. Edmonton: M.G. Hurtig, 1970. Hall's detailed and verbose account of his discovery of Frobisher relics, Inuit oral traditions, and eventually the Frobisher mine sites. This book is most profitably read as an example of high Victorian journalism and the literature of nineteenth-century exploration.

Hogarth, D.D., P.W. Boreham, and J.G. Mitchell. 1994. *Martin Frobisher's Northwest Venture, 1576–1581: Mines, Minerals & Metallurgy*. Hull: Canadian Museum of Civilization. A report on the geological and minerological analyses carried out by Donald Hogarth and his colleagues, this volume also contains information on the assaying, transport, and smelting of the Frobisher ores and a variety of related topics.

Kenyon, W.A. 1975. *Tokens of Possession: The Northern Voyages of Martin Frobisher*. Toronto: Royal Ontario Museum. An edited version (with modern spelling) of George Best's narratives of the three Frobisher voyages, together with a sparkling account of Kenyon's "Frobisher IV" expedition to Kodlunarn Island in 1974.

McDermott, James. 2001. *Martin Frobisher: Elizabethan Privateer*. New Haven: Yale University Press. The most complete and current biography of Frobisher, written by a leading scholar.

McFee, William. 1927. *The Life of Martin Frobisher*. New York: Harper and Brothers. The standard biography of Frobisher and still valuable despite the minor changes in interpretation which have resulted from recent research.

Quinn, A.M., and S. Hillier, eds. 1979. *New American World: a Documentary History of North America to 1612*. Vol. 3. New York: Arno Press. An accessible compilation of many of the original documents relating to New World exploration, this volume contains Michael Lok's 1576 outfitting accounts,

Christopher Hall's 1576 log, Dionyse Settle's narrative of the 1577 voyage, Thomas Ellis's 1578 journal, and the charges and countercharges between Lok and Frobisher in 1578.

Stefansson, Vilhjalmur, and Eloise McCaskill, eds. 1938. *The Three Voyages of Martin Frobisher*. London: Argonaut Press. Although this compilation of documents is not as complete as Collinson's, the collection is generally more accessible and contains many of the most important records relating to the Frobisher voyages. These include the narratives of George Best, Dionyse Settle, Richard Willes, Christopher Hall, Michael Lok, Thomas Ellis, and Edward Sellman, as well as related materials and a detailed analysis of the venture by Arctic explorer Stefansson.

Symons, T.H.B., ed. 1999. *Meta Incognita: A Discourse of Discovery*. Hull: Canadian Museum of Civilization. The twenty papers in these two volumes comprise the most significant result of the Meta Incognita Project. Prepared by an international group of historians, they present an extensive analysis of diverse aspects of the Frobisher venture. The large number of references cited in these papers provide an excellent starting point for anyone researching the subject and ensure that this publication will be a primary source for Frobisher research in the coming decades.

Index